POLITICAL THINKERS

POLITICAL THINKERS

VOLUME I
Hegel
Raymond Plant

VOLUME II
Edmund Burke: His Political Philosophy
Frank O'Gorman

VOLUME III
Karl Marx
Michael Evans

VOLUME IV
John Stuart Mill
R. J. Halliday

VOLUME V
Bentham
James Steintrager

VOLUME VI
Hobbes: Morals and Politics
D. D. Raphael

VOLUME VII
Aristotle
John B. Morrall

VOLUME VIII
John Locke
Geraint Parry

VOLUME IX
Plato
Robert W. Hall

POLITICAL THINKERS

General Editor: Geraint Parry

Volume V

Bentham

James Steintrager

Routledge
Taylor & Francis Group
LONDON AND NEW YORK

First published 1977
by George Allen & Unwin Ltd
This edition published 2004
by Routledge
2 Park Square, Milton Park, Abingdon, Oxon OX14 4RN
Simultaneously published in the USA and Canada by Routledge
by Routledge
711 Third Avenue, New York, NY 10017

Routledge is an imprint of the Taylor & Francis Group, an informa business

First issued in paperback 2012

Transferred to Digital Printing 2009

Typeset in Times by Keystroke, Jacaranda Lodge, Wolverhampton

British Library Cataloguing in Publication Data
A catalogue record for this book is available from the British Library

ISBN13: 978-0-415-32687-2 (hbk)
ISBN13: 978-0-415-61152-7 (pbk)

Publisher's Note

The publisher has gone to great lengths to ensure the quality of this reprint but points out that some imperfections in the original may be apparent.

BENTHAM

James Steintrager
Professor of Politics
at Wake Forest University

London
George Allen & Unwin Ltd
Ruskin House Museum Street

PREFACE

The present study was begun a number of years ago as the result of dissatisfaction with the accepted interpretations of Bentham's political thought, and in particular with the landmark criticisms by John Stuart Mill and Elie Halévy which set the tone for what one might call the standardised, textbook version. My dissatisfaction with that version, I soon discovered, was shared by others. Thus in my research and reflection I have benefited in many respects from the work of other Bentham scholars, even when I disagreed with their particular interpretations. A complete list of those whose work has been of use could not be culled from the bibliography of the present study since that, by necessity, has been kept selective. At the risk of failing to mention some who should be mentioned, I would cite, in particular, the works of C. W. Everett, C. K. Ogden, Mary Mack, David Baumgardt, H. L. A. Hart, David Manning, David Lyons, Bhikhu Parekh, Warren Roberts and J. H. Burns.

In contrast with many other revisionist interpretations, I am convinced that there is some truth in the older view, although I came to realise that even when it appeared to be correct the supporting evidence was often either weak or distorted. It became apparent at an early stage that to make a just statement about Bentham's political thought it would be necessary to examine the extensive manuscript collections which he left, especially those at University College, London, and in the British Museum. But I considerably underestimated the difficulty of that undertaking, given the quantity of the material, the illegible nature of Bentham's handwriting, and the problem of estimating the merits of material which was often fragmentary in nature. First in 1966–7, and again in 1968–9 and 1973–4, I worked through as many of the manuscripts as I could until I became convinced that the law of diminishing returns was clearly coming into play. I am quite aware of the fact that there are manuscripts which I did not examine, or which I did examine but, perhaps, without sufficient awareness of their significance. A complete examination, then, might lead to an interpretation somewhat different from that at which I arrived on certain points. My appreciation of this is only underlined by the fact that on several occasions manuscripts which I later realised were of considerable importance were not thought to be so when I first read them. The material on geometry discussed in Chapter I provides an excellent example of this, as do the many manuscripts on the obstacles which Bentham perceived stood in the way of reform in his early years, which are discussed in Chapter II. But a complete examination would take a lifetime longer than Bentham's, since I am convinced it would take more time to read what he wrote than it took him to write it!

With few exceptions the transcripts from Bentham's pinched writing are my own. It should be noted that in respect to punctuation, spelling, the use of italics and the dash, Bentham's usage was often uniquely his own. I have attempted to reproduce his usage as exactly as possible save on a very few occasions when I have silently corrected an obvious slip of the pen. What is true of the manuscripts is also true of his published writings, and the same policy has been followed in respect to them. Thus whenever italics are used, they are in the original. Finally, it should be added that throughout this study I have written of the English Constitution and England rather than of the British Constitution and Britain because, in general, that is what Bentham did.

An enterprise of this kind obviously incurs a great many obligations. I am indebted to a number of foundations and universities for the generous financial assistance which allowed me to travel to and live in London on the several occasions mentioned above. Wake Forest University, which granted me an R. J. Reynolds research leave and travel money, and the H. B. Earhart Foundation, which on two occasions supported my work, deserve my particular thanks. But I should also like to thank the Society for Religion in Higher Education, the American Philosophical Society and the University of Texas at Austin, as well as to acknowledge the assistance of the later Professor Leo Strauss and Professor Gerhart Niemeyer who helped me to secure these various grants. I am grateful to the University College Library, London, for permission to quote extensively from the Bentham Manuscript Collection. Mr J. W. Scott, the Library Director, Mrs J. Percival, as well as her predecessor, Miss Margaret Skerl, and the staff of the Library were most kind in the ways in which they assisted me. Similar thanks are due to the staffs of the Rare Manuscript Room of the British Museum and the British Library. Miss Jean Younger, my research assistant, and Mrs Emily Lincoln, typist, proofreader and friend, deserve special commendation for catching my all too frequent mistakes.

Over the past ten years I have greatly profited from the knowledge and guidance of Professor J. H. Burns of University College, who carefully listened to and commented on my interpretation of Bentham's political thought as it evolved over the years. Mr Charles Furth, of George Allen & Unwin, and Professor Geraint Parry, the general editor of the Political Thinkers series, deserve my gratitude not only for having invited me to write this study but for their extraordinary patience in awaiting its completion. Nothing can adequately serve to thank my parents, who at considerable personal sacrifice made it possible for me to have a university education. Finally, I wish to express my thanks to my children, Kirsten, Jimmy, Rebecca and Megan, for their patience and understanding; and above all to my wife, Marianne, herself trained in political philosophy, who not only encouraged me but provided thoughtful criticism of my work.

CONTENTS

Introduction

In 1768 Jeremy Bentham discovered the principle of utility, that the greatest happiness of the greatest number is the only proper measure of right and wrong and the only proper end of government. From then until his death in 1832, he worked with steadiness and determination to discover means of promoting that end and thus 'to rear the fabric of felicity by the hands of reason and of law'.[1] This dedicated reformer, however, was not one to take to the hustings. Instead he worked away in seclusion, turning out thousands upon thousands of manuscript pages on a wide variety of reform topics, and, in fact, seeing few of these projects through to completion by himself. Most often he would turn the manuscripts over to compatriots who had to make sense out of his pinched handwriting and bring order to the confusion of alternate readings, changed orderings and occasional gaps in the argument. Despite the rather curious way in which Bentham's writings on reform were published; despite the difficulty of his writing style which grew ever more cumbersome over the years; despite the fact that his views have been disproved countless times from his own day to the present; despite all this and more, Bentham's ideas profoundly altered the course of English politics during the nineteenth century. Indeed, it may truly be said that, as the late Sir Denis Brogan remarked, Benthamism remains one of the prevalent modes of thought among intellectuals and politicians in England even today.[2]

Bentham was born in London in 1748. His father, Jeremiah Bentham, was a prosperous man, a lawyer by profession but whose wealth came from property holdings rather than the practice of law. Jeremiah was an aggressive social climber. When Jeremy showed signs of exceptional ability, his father's hopes for social advancement soared. He imagined the lad rising to great heights as a barrister, perhaps even becoming Lord Chancellor; and he methodically pushed the boy academically (which was quite easy given his intelligence) and socially (which was quite difficult given his shyness and awkwardness). Jeremy was educated first by his father and a French tutor, and then sent to Westminster School. At the age of twelve he entered Queen's College, Oxford. By

1763, while only fifteen, he was admitted to Lincoln's Inn and began attending sittings of the King's Bench. The following year he received his Bachelor of Arts degree, and in 1767 he received the Master's degree. In 1769, having reached his majority, he was admitted to the practice of law. Thus it might appear that his father's hopes were to be realised. He was formally ready to enter upon a prosperous career in the law. It was a prospect not to be realised, for the seemingly chance discovery of the principle of utility deflected him from that course, and turned him from the practice of law as it was to the study of law as it ought to be.[3] This decision disappointed Jeremiah Bentham, who nevertheless grudgingly supported his son financially. To be sure, Jeremy was to achieve prestige, though long after his father's death in 1792; and it was not prestige within the establishment but as 'the great questioner of things established'.[4]

Bentham's first book, *A Fragment on Government* (1776), which his father justly admired, gave indications of things to come. It was a stinging criticism of one section of Sir William Blackstone's *Commentaries on the Laws of England*. The *Commentaries*, first published in 1765–9, was widely celebrated, as Bentham was anxious to point out, not least because it represented both the dominant view of English law and the accepted doctrine as to the nature of the English Constitution. Indeed, the section which Bentham singled out for attack, hoping thereby to discredit the work as a whole, was essentially a modified restatement of the Lockean theory of civil government. Bentham's criticisms did not necessarily constitute a rejection of the English Constitution, though they certainly amounted to a rejection of what he felt to be its confused and inadequate theoretical underpinnings; and, as he wrote in his own copy of the *Fragment*, 'this was the very first publication by which men at large were invited to break loose from the trammels of authority and ancestor-wisdom in the field of law'.[5] A similar confidence in the power of reason, or at least of his own reason, to dispel the mysteries and dogmatism of law and government marks all of Bentham's published writings. His best-known work, *An Introduction to the Principles of Morals and Legislation*, is an assertive (although remarkably brief) explication of the principle of utility, and a summary dismissal of all rival moral theories. In general, Bentham proceeded without any apparent hesitation to develop his own ideas, confident of their correctness and seemingly unaware of any complications or difficulties which might stand in the way of his attempt to establish on a firm footing, once and for all, a science of morals and legislation. As he himself suggested, he was to be the Newton of the moral world. His moral calculus would do for morals and legislation what the Newtonian calculus did for the laws of motion and the science of the physical world in general. With it, the legislator would be able to understand the tendencies of human actions towards and away from the end of the greatest happiness of the greatest number, and be able to employ appropriate sanctions to discourage undesirable tendencies and to encourage desirable ones.[6] Thus he would be like the physicist who is able to calculate the appropriate force needed to move a given mass in a desired direction. Indeed, Bentham even thought it would be possible to reduce the various circumstances, which might otherwise cause distortions in the calculations, to supplementary formulae, so that variations of time and place might be taken into account by the legislator in the same way as the physicist allows for such variables as friction and atmospheric pressure.[7] The legislator, then, would be able to know both what actions ought to be considered criminal, because they diminish the greatest happiness of the greatest number, and what penalties ought to be held up to those contemplating such criminal activities so as to convince them that it would not be worthwhile, in terms of their individual happiness, to do what they were contemplating. Bentham, then, appears to be a model of what Professor Michael Oakeshott has described so ably as 'Rationalism in Politics'.[8] Or as one of Bentham's own contemporaries suggested:

> Mr Bentham maintains, that in all cases we ought to disregard the presumptions arising from moral approbation, and, by a resolute and scrupulous analysis, to get at the naked utility upon which it is founded; and then, by the application of his new moral arithmetic, to determine its quantity, its composition, and its value, and, according to the result of this investigation to regulate our moral approbation for the future.[9]

Bentham's unabashed confidence in his new system, a confidence more than echoed by his followers, taken in the light of the epoch in which he wrote, has led to a fairly standard interpretation of him and of his enterprise. Though there are nuances and variations, the stock-in-trade argument comes down pretty much to the following: Bentham grew up in an era in which the natural sciences were making rapid strides, a fact of which he was deeply aware. The advancement of science was not merely theoretical. Theory was speedily transformed into those practical alterations which we now call collectively 'The Industrial Revolution'. The Industrial Revolution, along with other complex factors, was having a devastating effect on England, as a green and pleasant land became dotted with satanic mills. The yeoman farmer was uprooted. The day labourer became a factory worker. Cities grew in size. Traditional values and *mores* were shaken. Beginning at least as early as 1763, with the initial conflict between the King and John Wilkes, there were a series of political and constitutional struggles within the country, to say nothing of the struggle of the American colonies against the mother country. Successive governments seemed unwilling or unable to deal with the growing economic and social problems. Men no longer knew how to deal with one another. 'The absence of a sense of corporate existence made it very difficult for men to conceive of one another as anything but potential enemies.'[10] What was needed was a new moral and legislative code: 'a code for individuals who did not enjoy a shared inheritance, whose relationships were impersonal'.[11] It was a situation ready made for someone like Bentham. Trained in the law, he dabbled in science and was fascinated by technology. Dismayed by the moral, social, economic and political decay, he hoped to remedy the situation by imitating the method of the natural sciences. Newton had succeeded by founding on 'a single law a complete science of nature' and Bentham believed that he had found 'an analogous principle capable of serving for the establishment of a synthetic science of the phenomena of moral and social life'.[12] His confidence was born partly of his own belief in his genius and partly out of the crisis itself, for necessity is ever the mother of invention. Unfortunately, Bentham was devoid of practical experience, a fault made worse by his unwillingness to learn from others and his considerable disdain for history. As a recent reviewer of his early letters has asserted:

> Bentham's correspondence, in short, exhibits the same qualities that are evident in his formal writings – a pronounced insularity, self-containment, and self-satisfaction. It is as if, very early in his life, he had committed himself to a system of thought which he found entirely persuasive, totally comprehensive, and, not the least of its merits, uniquely his. Because that system was, for him, so unproblematic, so evidently true and sufficient for all purposes, he felt little need, in his public presentations of it, to take special note of either his forebears or his contemporaries. Still less in his private correspondence, with those he thought of as friends, did he feel the need to give expression to views that to him seemed perfectly obvious.[13]

Similar comments could be culled from any number of critics from Bentham's day until the present. Even his most famous disciple, John Stuart Mill, described him as 'one-eyed' and faulted his narrowness, his want of experience and his rigidity.[14] Despite the quite remarkable agreement of these critics with respect to the nature and genesis of Bentham's thought – an agreement which has made the interpretation the authorised textbook version – Bentham has also had his defenders who have argued strenuously that his thought was both more complex and more subtle than it is credited with being.[15] If these revisionists have not yet convinced the writers of textbooks and articles, they have at least shown that the standard interpretation is problematic and, in its own way, as one-sided as it accuses Bentham of having been.

That during Bentham's formative years, England experienced grave social, economic and political difficulties is beyond dispute. But the suggestion that Bentham seized upon the principle of utility in response to that crisis has never been satisfactorily demonstrated. Elie Halévy, who in this respect and many others sets the standard, asserted that 'Jeremy Bentham was born in 1748, and the smallest events of his childhood show that the period was one of transition and of stress. His father had been a Jacobite, but had ultimately rallied to the Hanoverian dynasty'.[16] When one turns, however, to the passage in John Bowring's *Memoirs of Bentham*, which Halévy cites, one discovers the following account:

> 'My grandfather on my father's side', writes Bentham, 'being a Jacobite, my father, *comme de raison*, was bred up in the same principles. My father subsequently, without much cost in conveyancing, transferred his adherence from the Stuarts to the Guelphs. A circumstance that gave no small facility to it was a matrimonial alliance that had been contracted by a relation of my mother's with a *valet de cambre* of George the Second's.'[17]

This is scarcely the stuff of which crises are made. The fact of the matter is that as one ponders Bentham's letters, manuscripts and books written during his formative years, one finds very little evidence that he himself felt that England was confronting any sort of disaster.

Bentham's formative years with respect to working out the initial implications of the principle of utility were from 1768 (when he discovered the principle) to 1780 (when the *Introduction to the Principles of Morals and Legislation* was, for the most part, completed and printed) or, perhaps, 1782 (by which time the manuscript for *Of Laws in General* was substantially completed).[18] Certainly he was well along in his work by 1785. But as Halévy himself recognised (although others have not been so aware of the fact), the first evidence one gets that Bentham thought England might be experiencing a constitutional crisis occurs around 1789 when he began reflecting on the French Revolution.[19] Bentham had certainly been interested in reform even before he became an adherent of the principle of utility. But for a very long time his overriding concern was with the reform of penal law and the judicial system. He felt that the confusions, uncertainties and obscurity of the penal law and its enforcement were causing the increasing crime rate which he saw afflicting the country. This is important to note, for there is a marked tendency to read into Bentham's thought causal factors for crime, such as socio-economic upheaval, which were not particularly on his mind.

Nor did he see any intrinsic reason why the English Constitution and Government should be unamenable to most of the changes which he felt ought to be made in criminal law and procedure. The English Constitution had its merits, even though the theory behind it was murky. What was most needed was not constitutional change but a change in attitude or mood. Bentham railed against Blackstone precisely because he represented and reinforced the widespread attitude that, so far as English Law and Government were concerned, everything was as it ought to be. Instead of such placid contentment and the 'common notion . . . that in the moral world there no longer remains any matter for *discovery*', what was needed was the restless, inquisitive and innovative mood which was characteristic of the natural sciences.[20] Precisely because he was influenced by the spirit of the natural sciences, however, Bentham was both optimistic about the possibility of improvement and experimental in his approach. Moral and legislative improvement could only be won by steady and dispassionate analysis which worked out in detail and proposed with caution the requisite changes. Here was no revolutionary. In fact, part of his criticism of Lockean constitutional theory was that its notions of a state of nature, a social contract and natural rights were dangerous fictions which might encourage reckless and revolutionary disobedience to the Municipal laws. Even the arch-anti-reformist Blackstone held that 'if any human law should allow or enjoin us' to transgress the natural or divine law then 'we are BOUND TO TRANSGRESS that human law, or else we must offend both the natural and divine'.[21] For the reform-minded Bentham such views were dangerous in the extreme, and as much to be avoided as the thoughtless complacency with things as they were. He described his own attitude in the following way: 'Under a government of laws, what is the motto of a good citizen? *To obey punctually; to censure freely*.'[22] In principle, at least, England was a government of law though certainly one which needed criticism.

There is, however, one exception to the general rule that Bentham did not experience any personal crisis during his formative years and that he did not feel there was anything critically wrong with the English Constitution. That exception is Bentham's attitude toward the Church of England and the role it played within the established form of government; and, more generally, the impact of religion as such on the life of men. There is considerable evidence of the deep distress Bentham experienced as a result of his religious upbringing: his melancholy at reading Dodsley's *Preceptor* and the contributions to it of that 'gloomy moralist' Samuel Johnson; his shock at the infidelity and hyprocrisy of 'religionists' at Oxford; above all the deep distress he experienced when he had to subscribe to the Thirty-Nine Articles of the Church of England.[23] As a consequence of these events, he developed a lifelong and deep-seated hostility to religion in general and toward the Church of England in particular. This hostility is significant because it is when he is discussing religion that Bentham shows most clearly his awareness of the blind, prejudice-ridden, irrational side of man. Religion was for him the great enemy of reason and religion had a powerful hold on governors and governed alike. 'In Locke there is scarce any thing but clear ideas. Accordingly at Oxford, in spite of his stature his name is kept as hush as possible. His notions, if we may believe certain Tutors, lead to Atheism – Certainly they lead to the exercise of reason.'[24] Bentham is notorious for teaching that rational calculation was not only a norm but a description of the way men act. Did he not explicitly say that there is nothing 'novel' or 'unwarranted' or 'useless' in his hedonic calculus; indeed that it is 'nothing but . . . the practice of mankind'?[25] Yet as one ponders the early manuscripts on religion one wonders at times whether he thought the great mass of men ever perceived their own interest since they were so blinded by the superstitions and fictions cultivated by religion. When, in the light of the manuscripts, one re-reads his bold claim that men do calculate, one sees what has seldom been noticed: the claim is qualified by the fact that Bentham adds 'wheresoever they have a clear view of their own interest', which comes very close to making the assertion tautological. Nor is it uninteresting to note that he gave but one example to show that men do calculate, and that concerned an exchange of property, a case where, indeed, one might well expect men to calculate with some care. Even in this case Bentham doubted that men can even estimate the intensity, the fecundity or the purity of the pleasure likely to be derived from the exchange in advance of its actual execution.[26] Hedonic calculation, on occasion, might be a description of the way men behave but it ought always to be the norm.

> There is no certainty in this calculation: difficult it is to make those calculations nor is there any certainty in them when made. Is it so? indeed it cannot be denied: but this may be boldly affirmed, that there is no other method bad as the chance may be which this method gives us of judging right; thus no other method is there that affords so good an one: and that any other mode of judging is good or bad in proportion as it approaches to or deviates from this. This and this alone is that which is capable of giving to the mind the full satisfaction which the subject is capable of affording.[27]

As one reads such passages, one begins to realise that Bentham's view of man's nature was more complex than is generally admitted, and that he was aware of difficulties which stood in the way of his project. To understand that project one must see it as he saw it. One must take his view of the events of his time and not the perspective of later historians or even of those contemporaries who viewed things differently from the way in which he did. That Bentham may frequently have misread the events of his time seems certainly to be the case. But it is his understanding of those events, however erroneous, which shaped not only his thought but his manner of presentation, points which will be demonstrated in the remainder of this study. One further word of caution is in order. This work is an exposition of the development and nature of Bentham's political thought. Quite naturally the discussion touches at times on that broad and complex ethical approach known as utilitarianism. Utilitarianism may have its origins in Bentham's thought, and many of the misconceptions about utilitarianism have their roots in misconceptions about Bentham. But utilitarianism is not reducible to nor simply identical with his views and, accordingly, it is not my intention here to make any estimate of the adequacies or inadequacies of utilitarianism in general.

Notes Introduction

1 Jeremy Bentham, *An Introduction to the Principles of Morals and Legislation*, ed. J. H. Burns and H. L. A. Hart (London, The Athlone Press, 1970), p. 11. Further references to this work will be cited as *IPML*.

2 Sir Denis Brogan, 'The Intellectual in Great Britain', *The Intellectual in Politics*, ed. H. Malcolm Macdonald (Austin, The Humanities Research Center of The University of Texas, 1966), p. 64.

3 The best brief introduction to Bentham's early development is C. W. Everett, *The Education of Jeremy Bentham* (New York, Columbia University Press, 1931). Precisely from whom Bentham first learned the principle of utility is not clear. In later years he attributed the discovery to a chance reading of a pamphlet by Joseph Priestley, but the early manuscripts frequently mention Helvetius and even Beccaria. See University College Bentham Manuscripts, Box 14, pp. 317–18 with Box 27, pp. 100, 144, 148; Box 70, p. 23; Box 159, p. 270; and Box 21, p. 11. Further references to this collection will be cited in the following manner: UC 21, p. 11.

4 John Stuart Mill, 'Bentham', *Essays on Ethics, Religion and Society* in the *Collected Works of John Stuart Mill*, vol. x (Toronto, University of Toronto Press, 1969), p. 78.

5 Quoted in *The Works of Jeremy Bentham*, ed. John Bowring, 11 vols (Edinburgh, William Tait, 1838–43), vol. 1, p. 260 (*A Fragment on Government*). The Bowring text reads 'on the field of law' which would appear to be a misprint or a misreading. Further references to the Bowring edition will be cited as *Works*.

6 UC 27, p. 2; UC 32, p. 158 and, in general, *IPML*.

7 *Works*, 1, pp. 169–94 (*Essay on the Influence of Time and Place in Matters of Legislation*).

8 Michael Oakeshott, *Rationalism in Politics and Other Essays* (London, Methuen, 1962), pp. 1–36. Also D. H. Manning, *The Mind of Jeremy*

Bentham (London, Longmans, Green, 1968) which uses the Oakeshottian approach in analysing Bentham's thought.

9 [Francis Jeffrey], *The Edinburgh Review*, vol. IV (April 1804), p. 12.

10 Manning, op. cit., p. 46.

11 ibid., p. 5.

12 Elie Halévy, *The Growth of Philosophic Radicalism*, trans. Mary Morris (Boston, Mass., The Beacon Press, 1955), p. 3.

13 Gertrude Himmelfarb, 'On Reading Bentham Seriously', *Studies in Burke and His Time*, vol. XIV (Winter 1972–3), pp. 185–6.

14 Mill, 'Bentham', op. cit., p. 94 and pp. 77–115 in general.

15 For example Mary Mack, *Jeremy Bentham: An Odyssey of Ideas 1748–1792* (London, Heinemann, 1962).

16 Halévy, op. cit., p. 5.

17 *Works*, X, p. 2.

18 For an account of the history of *IPML* see the editorial Introduction, pp. xxxvii–xxxix and Bentham's own Preface, *IPML*, pp. 1–5; for *Of Laws in General*, ed. H. L. A. Hart (London, The Athlone Press, 1970), editorial Introduction, pp. xxxi–xlii. Further references to the latter work will be cited as *OLG*.

19 Halévy, op. cit., pp. 142–8, 164–77.

20 *Works*, I, p. 227 and pp. 227–39 in general (*A Fragment on Government*).

21 Sir William Blackstone, *Commentaries on the Laws of England* quoted in *Works*, I, pp. 286–7 (*A Fragment on Government*). For an attack on Locke's theory of government see UC 100, pp. 104–13.

22 *Works*, I, p. 230.

23 *Works*, X, pp. 13, 37, 39. For a more detailed account of Bentham's attitude toward religion see my 'Morality and Belief: The Origin and Purpose of Bentham's Writings on Religion', *The Mill News Letter*, VI (Spring 1971), pp. 3–15.

24 UC 96, p. 121.

25 *IPML*, pp. 40–1.

26 ibid. Also UC 141, p. 43.

27 UC 69, p. 198.

Chapter I

The Metaphysics of Jurisprudence

Bentham claimed that he took up the study of law for the only reason it was ever pursued in England, namely, to make money. He soon discovered the 'melancholy and unhappily but too indisputable a truth that in England [more] instances happen of Theft, Robberies & other crimes of indigence (Murder out of the question) than in any other country in Europe'.[1] The rising crime rate meant ever-increasing unhappiness for an ever-increasing number, victims and culprits alike; to say nothing of those who feared they might suffer because of the general atmosphere of insecurity. Bentham himself suffered at the sufferings of others because the sentiment of sympathy was strong in his nature. He was particularly distressed because, as he saw it, so much of the unhappiness was unnecessary. Although the fact of indigence might contribute to the crime rate, the real difficulty was the slow development of an appropriate art and science of legislation. He frequently compared legislation with medicine. It was, however, the art and science of healing on a grand scale, of ministering to the sickness of the body politic.[2]

Bentham's diagnosis of the sickness of the English body politic centred on his analysis of the English common law. Under the common law men often committed crimes because they did not even know that the activity which they pursued was criminal. Even when they did know, they might still pursue the course of action either because the penal sanctions levelled against the crime were insufficient to deter them, or because the application of those sanctions was erratic and uncertain. Heinous crimes went unpunished or were often only lightly punished. Indifferent acts were punished, often with severity. Acts rightly classified as offences were punished without due regard to the nature of the crime or the circumstances in which the crime was committed. Once a case came to trial there were many obstacles to obtaining a speedy and fair conclusion. The rules of evidence were highly technical and unnecessarily complicated. Useful evidence was precluded on obscure or even absurd grounds. The system of procedure in the courts caused cases to be spun out for years which, along with law taxes and legal fees, effectively prevented a great many subjects from receiving just treatment. Neither the rights nor duties of the citizens were well defined, and the law was not properly promulgated. Under the common law system judges were guided by precedents, but these precedents were collected, at best, in obscure books which were frequently written in Latin and inaccessible to anyone except judges and lawyers. Such laws were as good as no laws at all. There was no way in which the general public could know what the law was. Even if one could afford to consult a lawyer, one could still not be certain about the legal status of an act, for the precedents were not always consistent with one another. It was always possible for an opposing lawyer or a judge to come up with a ruling more obscure than usual, thus transforming an apparently legal act into an illegal one. In the common law, 'a great perhaps the greatest part of the business is done in the way of *ex post facto* law'.[3] Such a law might be suitable for 'those who neither know how to write, nor how to speak', that is to say 'for brutes'.[4] Yet in England it was what passed for the rule of law.

The task which Bentham set for himself was that of remedying these deficiencies. He did not believe that the reformation of the penal system would mean the end of crime. There would still be crimes and, as a result, unhappiness. There would also be unhappiness which was beyond the power of law to prevent. But there could be a substantial reduction in the level of unhappiness simply be reducing the common law to statutes, and by vigorously and systematically promulgating those statutes. To make the law known it was necessary to set it down in such a way that anyone of ordinary intelligence could discover with relative ease whether any statute forbade or in any way touched upon any course of activity the person might be considering: 'In a map of the law executed upon such a plan there are no *terrae incognitae*, no blank spaces: nothing is at least omitted, nothing unprovided for: the vast and hitherto shapeless expanse of jurisprudence is collected and condensed into a compact sphere which the eye at a moment's warning can traverse in all imaginable directions.'[5] Given such a systematic presentation of the law, the legal code might be easily divided into sections so that individuals involved in particular activities would have ready at hand a digest of the laws particularly applicable to them. Thus a publican or the operator of a turnpike, for example, could be required to have in his possession the digest of the laws applying to his trade – and Bentham actually set about drawing up examples of such digests.[6]

In order to achieve the end of remedying the defects of English law, an appropriate system of classifying offences was needed. No such classificatory system could be found in the works of men like Coke and Blackstone, for their writings were as confused and complicated as the common law itself. On the other hand, Bentham felt that great advances had been made in the natural sciences precisely because men like Linnaeus and Tobias Bergmann had introduced suitable systems of classification. Although Bentham was not uncritical of their efforts, he sought to imitate their success by devising a system of classification for jurisprudence.[7] Such a system must be comprehensive and complete. It must excite both the judgement and the memory so that 'the subject learns how he is benefitted, at the same time that he sees how he is restrained'.[8] 'This can only be done in the way of *bipartition*, dividing each superior branch into two, and but two, immediately subordinate ones; beginning with the logical whole, dividing that into two parts, then each of those parts into two others; and so on.'[9] Bentham practised what he preached. His manuscripts and books are filled with remarks on the theory of classification (although it would be years before he formally presented the theory on its own)[10] and with attempts to divide offences according to the method of bipartition or bifurcation in order to achieve a thorough and accurate map of the law. This penchant for classification dominated his work. The longest chapter by far in the *Introduction to the Principles of Morals and Legislation* is that on the 'Division of Offences', which is almost one third of the entire work. Nor is it the only chapter in the book where the concern for classification prevailed. This aspect of his work was not lost on his contemporaries. As a reviewer of the *Traités de Législation* (which was edited from Bentham's manuscripts by Etienne Dumont) remarked: 'In multiplying these distinctions and divisions which form the basis of his system, Mr Bentham appears to us to bear less resemblance to a philosopher of the present times, than to one of the old scholastic doctors who substituted classification for reasoning, and looked upon the ten categories as the most useful of all human inventions.'[11] It was a criticism which had occurred to Bentham himself. In an early manuscript, he remarked that while the schoolmen were criticised for the multitude of their divisions, that was not their failing. Their error was that they had 'nothing to divide'.[12]

The schoolmen, and the ancient Greeks who were their masters, had nothing to divide or to classify because they knew nothing of the fundamental nature of definition. They spoke of definition but they did not understand that the correct process of definition was the resolution of complex ideas into their component simple ones. The schoolmen did not even know what a simple idea was, for they had not grasped the distinction between real and fictitious entities. They were confused and they confused others by erroneously believing there were real objects which corresponded to abstract words. The error of the schoolmen was the error of English law and English lawyers. English jurisprudence abounded in fictions:

> Power, right, prohibition, duty, obligation, burthen, immunity, exemption, privilege, property, security, liberty – all these with a multitude of others that might be named are so many fictitious entities which the law upon one occasion or another is considered in common speech as creating or disposing of. Not an operation does it ever perform, but it is considered as creating or in some manner or other disposing of these its imaginary productions. All this it is plain is the mere work of the fancy: a kind of allegory: a riddle of which the solution is not otherwise to be given than by giving the history of the operations which the law performs in that case with regard to certain real entities.[13]

Because the common law was filled with such fictions, it would not be possible to end all the existing defects merely by turning the common law into adequately classified and promulgated statutory law. The language of the law also must be transformed. 'All questions of Law are no more than questions concerning the import of words. Questions the solution of which depend upon skill in Metaphysics.'[14] Thus, in addition to the schemes for classification, Bentham's early manuscripts abound with ideas for a 'vocabulary of the terms of Universal Jurisprudence with definitions disposed in a chain, consisting of sounds importing simple ideas' which would replace the technical, ambiguous, obscure and fictitious language of English jurisprudence.[15] This alteration was not merely methodical; it was metaphysical. It was rooted in the distinction between real and fictitious entities, so much so that Bentham tentatively entitled his work *Metaphysics of Jurisprudence*.[16]

Despite this fact, Elie Halévy held that 'the whole force of [Bentham's] criticism is concentrated not on the principles of metaphysics but on the established institutions, as a source of corruption and oppression'.[17] In more recent years, C. K. Ogden strenuously argued the importance and originality of Bentham's contributions toward understanding the linguistic basis of philosopy. But he also maintained that Bentham's work on the *Introduction to the Principles of Morals and Legislation* was not completed in 1780 because of the 'lack of an adequate foundation for his Theory of Fictions', an inadequacy which Ogden held was not corrected until the second decade of the nineteenth century.[18] Now it is the case that Bentham's early manuscripts do reveal, as Halévy argued, a certain disdain for metaphysical subtlety. He brushed aside Bishop Berkeley's arguments by assuming the existence of the material world 'without scruple, notwithstanding it has been the subject of so much controversy. I assume it boldly for this reason: because in point of practice, no bad consequences can possibly arise from supposing it to be true and the worst consequences can not but arise from supposing it to be false.'[19] It is also the case, as Ogden argued, that Bentham's views of the relationship of language to metaphysics, of words to things, and of the nature of language itself are not always worked out in a satisfactory manner. He is quite capable of condemning the obscurantist and technical language of the law for being remote from popular usage, which one should follow so far as possible, while at the same time coining what he himself called 'uncouth and formidable' neologisms. He can criticise popular speech for being too 'subtle', yet suggest that in order to obtain the closest approximation to the real entity for which a word stood one would have to trace the original meaning of the word to primitive times. He can proclaim that the season of fictions is over, that fictions will no longer be needed, and then argue that fictitious language is necessary if there is to be any communication between men at all.[20] But most, perhaps all, of these points may be made with equal validity about his later formulation of the theory of fictions. In general, C. W. Everett's suggestion that Bentham's 'later writings were either completions of plans sketched in his early years, or works published then which it would have been dangerous to avow earlier, or applications to contemporary political or legal situations of views arrived at in youth or early manhood',[21] is a good rule of thumb.

Certainly there are frequent discussions of fictions in the early manuscripts, although with the notable exception of an incomplete essay in the form of a letter to D'Alembert, Bentham seldom sustained the analysis for more than a page or two at a time. But, entirely aside from the fact that this is characteristic of the early manuscripts irrespective of the subject under discussion, what seems to have contributed greatly to his failure to present the theory of fictions thematically, as well as his failure to work out all of its implications for jurisprudence, was his concern over the dull and tedious character of such metaphysical analysis. He was convinced that the linguistic–metaphysical foundation for penal reform was essential, but he did not see how any but the most avid disciple would be willing to follow him. As he wrote to Morellet in 1789 concerning the *Introduction to the Principles of Morals and Legislation*: 'Several of my friends say that it contains all truth: but no man conceives it possible for any other man to get through it.'[22] Yet in a certain sense the *Introduction to the Principles of Morals and Legislation*, and the *Fragment on Government* were already compromises. Elements of Bentham's theory frequently appear in these two works although, characteristically, tucked away in Bentham's enormous footnotes. Thus, in the *Fragment*, when Bentham presented his theory of definition, he commenced with a warning that no one ought to trouble himself with the note 'who is not used, or does not intend to use himself to what are called *metaphysical* speculations'. He then went on to explain how legal fictions ought to be defined:

> For expounding the words *duty*, *right*, *power*, *title*, and those other terms of the same stamp that abound so much in ethics and jurisprudence, either I am much deceived, or the only method by which any instruction can be conveyed, is that which is here exemplified. An exposition framed after this method I would term *paraphrasis*.
>
> A word may be said to be expounded by *paraphrasis*, when not that *word* alone is translated into other *words*, but some whole *sentence*, of which it forms a part, is translated into another *sentence*; the words of which latter are expressive of such ideas as are *simple*, or are more immediately resolvable into simple ones than those of the former. Such are those expressive of *substances* and *simple modes*, in respect of such *abstract* terms as are expressive of what Locke has called *mixed modes*. This, in short, is the only method in which any abstract terms can, at the long run, be expounded to any instructive purpose; that is, in terms calculated to raise *images* either of *substances* perceived, or of emotions; – sources, one or other of which every idea must be drawn from, to be a clear one.[23]

Real entities are those things which can be directly perceived by the senses, and which occur either as states of mind or states of body.[24] In jurisprudence what must be done is to render intelligible such terms as 'power' and 'right' by analysing them in terms of real entities. To solve the riddle of knowing 'what it is that the law really does in every case, and in what condition it leaves the parties that are concerned', one must 'know in each case the acts which it takes into contemplation, and the aspect which it bears to them'.

> He must know who the persons, and what the things, if any, which are in question: what the acts are of those persons, whether for their termination they look to other persons or to things: and in what circumstances if in any the act if prohibited or permitted, commanded or left uncommanded. Knowing thus much, we shall have ideas to our words: not knowing it, we shall have none.[25]

The task of metaphysics, then, is to render clear to us what it is we really mean when we use certain words. Without such clarity, men will remain slaves to authority and to the customs of barbaric times.

Bentham's interest in the difference between fictitious and real entities, then, was not a matter of mere words. It was an integral part of his hopes for the reform of law, a reform intended to promote the happiness of the people. He was convinced that the failure to recognise the fictitious nature of crucial ethical and jurisprundential terms was not only the source of misfortune in the area of criminal law, but also the root cause of much political conflict. 'Till men are sufficiently aware of the ambiguity of words, political discussions may be carried on continually, without profit and without end.'[26] It is well to recall that the *Fragment on Government* was an attack on the obscurity of Blackstone's sentences, terminology and definitions (or, rather, the want of any genuine definitions); and that Bentham felt that Blackstone's use of fictions and obscurantist language was a purposeful attempt to subdue the spirit of reformation.[27] Indeed, to speak of the common law itself as if it were a real law was at the crux of the matter, for it was impossible to know what person actually made the law or to which persons it applied. But Bentham's position is perhaps made clearer by focusing on the revolutionary activity for which fictions also were employed. The controversy with the American colonies, for example, turned very largely on the meaning of words. Thus the two sides used the same terms, such as 'consent', 'liberty', 'representation' or 'taxation', to mean quite different things, without either side perceiving that this was what was happening. Such confusion could only be remedied by referring the two different usages to real entities; by seeking, as one might say, the metaphysical foundations of the terms. The dispute with the colonies showed both that this was a difficult task and that it was profoundly dangerous to fail to attempt it. The English Government, for example, claimed that the colonies were represented in Parliament, and thus had no cause to complain about the taxes which had been levied. But the colonies could rightly ask where the *real* persons were who represented them. The colonists, for their part, spoke of a natural right to representation. But the mother country could rightly ask where the real person was who gave them that right. Rights are only created by laws, and laws are the activity of human beings. Yet because of such abuses of language, England and the colonies were on the brink of war – a war which Bentham, in one of his megalomanic moods, thought might be avoided if only he could complete his dictionary of moral and jurisprudential terms in time![28]

It is evident, given his awareness of how difficult his new metaphysical language of jurisprudence was, that Bentham knew that issues could not be resolved so easily. Moreover, he also knew that there could be disagreements over facts, not words, and 'unhappily the power of Metaphysics can do but little' to resolve such disputes, particularly 'so long as that be true in sober sadness which David said in his wrath, All men are lyars'.[29] Even if one could adequately develop a suitable grammar for politics, there would be more than a few difficulties involved in getting it accepted, for, where men's interests and passions are involved, there is always difficulty in seeing that reason prevails.[30] Bentham may be been optimistic about reason ultimately prevailing, but he was not simple-minded in his optimism and he knew the realms of politics and morality were particularly prone to the influence of passion and interest.

What is more important to note for present purposes is that for Bentham there were two different types of fictions or, to speak more accurately, there were fictional entities and fabulous entities. It was the latter which had to be purged from jurisprudence while the former needed only to be established on firmer foundations. Legal rights were fictional entities, and Bentham did not deny that they had an important place in political life. Quite the contrary, life would be intolerable without them. Natural rights, in contrast, were fabulous entities. They were akin to the chimeras of the poets. Unfortunately, the language of law was infested with such entities. In ages past the office of the legislator frequently coincided with the office of the poet, and, in consequence, the spirit of poetry dominated the study and practice of legislation.

> The end of poetic language and the end of legal language are precisely opposite. The end of the Poet is to throw the mind into a kind of pleasing delirium which disturbs the exercise of the judgement, and is favoured by the indistinctness of the images offered to the conception. The purpose of the legislator requires that both the composer and the reader be as much as possible in their sober senses that they may be able (the one for the purpose of determining what he shall command, the other for that of knowing what he is to obey) to distinguish every object as perfectly as possible from all others with which it is in danger of being confounded. No kind of enthusiasm ought either the Legislator or the Judge to have about them, not even the enthusiasm of humanity.[31]

To achieve such composure would be difficult. But even if it could be achieved, would it not be an endless task to purify the language of even one country, defining by paraphrasis the fictions and purging the fabulous entities? 'Now of the infinite variety of nations there are upon the earth, there are no two which agree exactly in their laws: certainly not in the whole; perhaps not even in any single article; and let them agree today, they would disagree tomorrow.'[32] Yet Bentham was proposing the establishment of a universal jurisprudence, since it would be quite mad to speak of a metaphysics for one country. Bentham's response to this difficulty seems to have been twofold. First, there are certain terms such as power, right, obligation and liberty which 'in all languages are pretty exactly correspondent to one another: which comes to the same thing nearly as if they were the same'.[33] Second, he conceived of his function as that of a censor, one who discusses the law as it ought to be, and not as an historian, one who discusses the law as it is. Universal jurisprudence is censorial. It criticises the law as it is in the light of what the law ought to be, and what ought to be ultimately transcends the boundaries of any given nation.[34] To censor means to appeal to some standard, some measure of what ought to be, and Bentham's appeal was, of course, to the principle of utility.

Bentham's explanation of the principle of utility is as remarkable for its brevity as it is for its confident tone. The fourteen slight sections entitled 'Of the Principle of Utility', the opening chapter of the *Introduction to the Principles of Morals and Legislation*, constitute almost his only attempt to give 'an explicit and determinate account' of the foundations of his system. The principle of utility 'approves or disapproves of every action whatsoever, according to the tendency which it appears to have to augment or diminish the happiness of the party whose interest is in question', and happiness is to be measured in hedonic terms: 'a thing is said to promote the interest, or to be *for* the interest, of an individual, when it tends to add to the sum total of his pleasures: or, what comes to the same thing, to diminish the sum total of his pains'.[35] In swift strokes such expressions as the 'interest of the community', 'ought' and 'ought not' are explained, and the rectitude of the principle is asserted with the following haughty remark:

> Has the rectitude of this principle been ever formally contested? It should seem that it had, by those who have not known what they have been meaning. Is it susceptible of any direct proof? it should seem not: for that which is used to prove every thing else, cannot itself be proved: a chain of proofs must have their commencement somewhere. To give such proof is as impossible as it is needless.[36]

Seldom in the thousands and thousands of pages he was to write in subsequent years did Bentham do more than to refer to these remarks in the opening chapter of the *Introduction*. Seldom did he offer any further explanation. Quite understandably, then, that chapter has become the focal point for the criticism levelled at him, and commentator after commentator has tried to explain what Bentham meant and to show why he was wrong. Understandable as this is, it has unfortunately led to considerable misinterpretation and confusion.

Bentham's self-assurance has led to the widely held view that he embraced the principle of utility rather unthinkingly or in a dogmatic manner, and that he was oblivious to what must appear to others as obvious difficulties. Halévy, for example, wondered 'whether Bentham did not found his doctrine on elementary principles, whose real obscurity and complexity, as now revealed to us by the study of their historical development, he failed to understand . . . He liked to think that he had discovered in the principle of utility a simple positive principle on which all men would be able to agree so as to reform society on a systematic plan; and this belief, when once formed, strengthened in him his taste for theoretic simplification joined with a passion for practical reform.'[37] Similar remarks could be quoted from a great number of other critics, though to do so would be tedious and would produce only a series of mildly variant critiques. Yet for all that, the fact is that as one studies the early manuscripts and, indeed, the books when viewed in the light of the manuscripts, one begins to realise that Bentham did have his doubts. Above all one sees that he found the principle of utility attractive because of its heuristic nature. The principle of utility was meant to generate a system, but it was intended to be an open system, one characterised by flexibility and development through the medium of rational discourse.

Bentham's general complaint against all ethical systems other than utilitarianism is that they are dogmatic, that they are but 'so many contrivances for avoiding the obligation of appealing to any external standard, and for prevailing upon the reader to accept the author's sentiment or opinion as a reason, and that a sufficient one for itself' as to the morality or immorality of any given action.[38] Whether the appeal is to a moral sense, common sense, a rule of right reason, a law of nature, or any similar phrase as the standard, the adherents of such systems are, in fact, only appealing to their own opinion. They seek to close all discussion with an *ipse dixit*. In contrast, the principle of utility seeks to open discussion about the morality or immorality of a given action and to settle that discussion by appealing to an external standard, namely, the feelings of those real persons whose interests will be affected by the consequences of the action. When a person condemns an action on the grounds that it violates the principle of utility, he is saying that the action diminishes the greatest happiness of the greatest number. He too is asserting an opinion, but it is an opinion which can be tested. Ultimately it must be tested by asking, in some way, those who will be or might be affected whether, in their judgement, the action appears to them to be advantageous or detrimental to their own happiness; and by then summing up the feelings of the parties concerned. There is no other standard but the judgement of the individuals concerned. There is no appeal to such abstractions as the common good or the national welfare or the wellbeing of the community.

> The interest of the community is one of the most general expressions that can occur in the phraseology of morals: no wonder that the meaning of it is often lost. When it has a meaning, it is this. The community is a fictitious *body*, composed of the individual persons who are considered as constituting as it were its *members*. The interest of the community then is, what? – the sum of the interests of the several members who compose it.[39]

Moreover, Bentham made two important assumptions. First, each person is to count for one and only for one in making the assessment. Second, there is no pleasure, no matter how heinous it might seem to a given person, which ought to be condemned without a hearing. Any pleasure, taken in itself, is a good for the individual who experiences it. If it is to be condemned as criminal or immoral, it must be shown that it is detrimental to the happiness of others who are affected. The burden of proof is on those who would prohibit any pleasure-producing activity. They must show that it would cause definite and assignable pains to definite and assignable persons (or classes of persons), and that that pain would outweigh the pleasure of the person or persons who are pursuing it. This judgement must be made in terms of the consequences of the action to others, and never on the basis of a claim that the action does injury to the actor himself. Each man alone can judge whether or not the pleasure he purchases is worth the pain he himself pays. To forbid someone from doing something which only does harm to himself is, at least as far as the law is concerned, a superfluous work. Bentham, in fact, believed that a number of activities at that time condemned as criminal, including usury, sexual activities such as pederasty, sodomy and fornication, and unorthodox religious beliefs and practices, ought not to be forbidden in any system of law guided by the principle of utility. As the unpublished manuscripts in particular testify, he ardently hoped for a degree of religious and sexual freedom beyond what is yet the common legal practice; and he did so because he believed it would contribute to the greatest happiness of the greatest number.[40] In Bentham's eyes one of the appeals of the principle of utility was its profoundly liberating potential.

There is no disputing the many difficulties which would confront any consistent attempt to employ Bentham's hedonic calculus even in a relatively small community. Strictly speaking, it would be impossible even on his own terms since he consistently admitted that one of the elements to be considered in measuring the value of pleasure, namely, intensity, could not be assigned any value or, at best, a nominal one. It is doubtful whether Bentham ever expected the calculus to be strictly and consistently applied, although he certainly believed that it was a fruitful model for the legislator, and, as we saw at the end of the *Introduction*, that the more closely it was approximated the more likely it would be that the greatest happiness of the greatest number would result. Bentham's model must be judged, at least in part, by the practices of English law in his day, for it must not be forgotten that there was much senseless brutality in the laws of England, such as the savage punishment of poachers and the indiscriminate use of the death penalty. Still, there are serious problems with Bentham's argument, not the least of which is the discrepancy between the type of information needed to make an accurate estimate of the greatest happiness of the greatest number, and the type of person Bentham thought was qualified to make such an estimation. In arguing that a given activity could be considered beneficial or detrimental to the community only by consulting the feelings of the individuals affected, Bentham, in effect, had built a potentially democratic element into his theory. But, at this stage of his career, he did not feel that this engendered any need for a democratic electoral system. While the legislator ought to consult public opinion in some manner or another (and Bentham is not very specific as to how this would be done), the truth is that Bentham believed that the great majority of men are far too busy to calculate on most matters of public importance, and, furthermore, they lack the ability to do so. The legislative art demands great skill. There are no short cuts in discovering what constitutes the greatest happiness of the greatest number. Many pleasures and pains are complex and it takes considerable analysis to discover what their constituent parts are. Yet such analysis is necessary if one is to succeed in increasing pleasure and decreasing pain in the community. This task must be conducted in the best scientific spirit, through close observation of experience and, when possible, through experimentation. 'Politics not less than Physics is an experimental science: feelings not words are the elements that comprise it.'[41] One cannot know whether actions are pleasant or painful by consulting allegedly authoritative books (among which Bentham especially included the Bible as well as Blackstone) but only by examining the feelings of the people. To be sure, while Bentham clearly wished to challenge some existing laws, he admitted there were longstanding rules of law which the legislator would do well to follow, although always with the understanding that, at any time in the future, reassessment of their utility might be required. By retaining longstanding rules, apparently sufficiently shown by experience to be useful, the legislator's task would be made easier. He would not have to begin *de novo*. Still, the work of the legislator was truly formidable in Bentham's eyes, and certainly beyond the capacity of most men. Of course, the establishment of a proper methodology, a correct system of nomenclature and classification, would make the work easier, but nomenclature and classification would remain subordinate to observation and experience. It would be no mean accomplishment to establish an appropriate system of nomenclature and of classification, but even if they were established it would be difficult to employ them properly. 'He will repeat it boldly (for it has been said before him), truths that form the basis of political and moral science, are not to be discovered but by investigations as severe as mathematical ones, and beyond all comparison more intricate and extensive . . . There is no *King's Road*, no *Stadtholder's Gate*, to legislative, any more than to mathematic science.'[42] Just as few are truly skilled in the theory and practice of mathematics and physics, so too few would be truly skilled in the political and moral science.

It is misleading, then, to suggest that Bentham underestimated the complexity of analysis that would be required to employ the principle of utility, or to claim that he had a taste for theoretic simplification, or to hold that he believed his approach was unproblematic. Still, if the science of morals and legislation, founded upon the principle of utility, would involve investigations as severe as mathematical ones, what of the principle itself? Bentham maintained that it, in contrast, was self-evident and could only be contested 'by those who have not known what they have been meaning'.[43] By comparing the *Introduction to the Principles of Morals and Legislation* to a work in pure mathematics, he certainly created the impression that he was treating the principle of utility as if it had the same status in the moral world which the axioms of geometry have in the mathematical one. Unless a person is of very mean capacity, he can grasp the validity of the axioms of geometry as soon as he understands the meaning of the terms employed. With a little more effort, he can come to understand the deductions which are made employing the axioms. Acting like a geometrician, Bentham not only presented his moral principle as an axiom, but he introduced a supporting psychological statement (that pain and pleasure determine us to do what we do) as if it also was self-evident. Nor did he stop there. Other corollary moral and psychological statements are presented without any attempt at proof, as if they were either self-evident or obvious deductions from the basic moral and psychological axioms.[44]

There is no gainsaying that Bentham left himself open to the charge that he wrongly perceived as axiomatic both moral and psychological statements which are far from being self-evident. Thinkers of more than ordinary capability have denied that happiness is the only measure of right and wrong, and they have especially done so when happiness is measured only in terms of pleasure or the absence of pain. Yet Bentham seemed oblivious to such opposition and apparently took for granted the geometric-like certitude of the axioms he advanced. It is interesting, then, to discover that in manuscripts on the subject of geometry, written between 1773 and 1776, Bentham maintained that while there was general concurrence in the postulates of geometry, it would be difficult indeed to find a similar concurrence over moral postulates. This was because the terms and ideas in morals are so much more complex than those in geometry, and because 'interest & passion' prevent moral postulates from being 'generally perceived'.[45] Geometry, he argued, was a treacherous model for the science of morals and legislation for it leads one to expect simple solutions for difficult problems, and a degree of certitude which is not possible in such a controversial area. Indeed, he maintained that it was wrong to believe that the axioms of geometry had always been accepted as self-evident. The principles of geometry, like the principles of every other art or science, could only have been derived from experience, and he speculated that there must have been disputes over the validity of what comes down to us only in a mature and authoritative form in Euclid. Indeed, Bentham was quite prepared to doubt even the authority of Euclid since no man is infallible. Geometry is capable of a high degree of certitude in its axioms and operations, but this is due to its relatively simple nature and not to the excellence of the discipline. Just as geometry is far more certain in its pronouncements and far easier to learn, so too it is of far less utility than less certain and more complex disciplines such as chemistry, mechanics, moral science and jurisprudence. Whatever other utility Bentham's views on geometry might have, they clearly show that he did not see in it a particularly fruitful model for the art and science of morals and legislation.

There is a curious difference, then, between what Bentham wrote about geometry in the manuscripts, and the way he appears to proceed in the *Introduction to the Principles of Morals and Legislation*, to say nothing of other writings. It would be convenient if one could argue that he put aside his youthful doubts about geometry being a useful model for morals and legislation but, in fact, those doubts are repeated in manuscripts written as late as 1831.[46] Before considering more fully the implications of this fact, there is another argument frequently made against Bentham which must be considered, and that is the argument that he thought he had given an inductive proof for the principle of utility by basing moral hedonism on what is known as psychological hedonism. The opening passage of the *Introduction* is certainly one of the most discussed remarks which Bentham ever made:

> Nature has placed mankind under the governance of two sovereign masters, *pain* and *pleasure*. It is for them alone to point out what we ought to do, as well as to determine what we shall do. On the one hand the standard of right and wrong, on the other the chain of causes and effects, are fastened to their throne. They govern us in all we do, in all we say, in all we think: every effort we can make to throw off our subjection, will serve but to demonstrate and confirm it. In words a man may pretend to abjure their empire: but in reality he will remain subject to it all the while. The *principle of utility* recognizes this subjection, and assumes it for the foundation of that system, the object of which is to rear the fabric of felicity by the hands of reason and of law. Systems which attempt to question it, deal in sounds instead of sense, in caprice instead of reason, in darkness instead of light.[47]

Psychological hedonism maintains that men are governed in all their actions by the inevitable and invariable necessity of choosing pleasure and avoiding pain. Bentham apparently used this 'scientific law' to teach 'at one and the same time what is and what ought to be'.[48] But is not this a *petitio principii* of the first order? Had not Hume complained against 'every system of morality' for moving from propositions connected with '*is*, and *is not*' to those connected 'with an *ought*, or an *ought not*'?

> This change is imperceptible; but is, however, of the last consequence. For as this *ought*, or *ought not*, expresses some new relation or affirmation, 'tis necessary that it shou'd be observ'd and explain'd; and at the same time that a reason should be given, for what seems altogether inconceivable, how this new relation can be a deduction from others, which are entirely different from it.[49]

Bentham's shift from an 'is' to an 'ought' can hardly be described as 'imperceptible'. When one considers that Bentham claimed that Hume's *Treatise* was the work of a 'penetrating and acute metaphysician' and that upon reading it he 'felt as if the scales had fallen from [his] eyes'; and that, in later years, he praised the passage quoted from Hume as one of the most perceptive of remarks,[50] his own failure to abide by Hume's dictum without offering any reason seems quite amazing. Yet Bentham never disclaimed the opening paragraph of the *Introduction to the Principles of Morals and Legislation*; he republished it unaltered and unexplained late in his life; and he constantly referred to the passage in his other writings without a second thought about its validity.

Two remarks in the *Introduction* itself make Bentham's procedure less curious than might otherwise seem to be the case. In the first place, the controversial opening paragraph is followed by a one-sentence paragraph which completes the opening numbered section: 'But enough of metaphor and declamation: it is not by such means that moral science is to be improved.'[51] This second, qualifying remark has been almost universally ignored, and this despite the fact that Bentham was strident in his warnings about the use of metaphors and declamation in the moral and legislative sciences. He consistently held that metaphors were substitutes for reasons. They confuse when there is a need for clarity. They offer men sounds instead of sense. Despite such criticisms, Bentham himself resorted to metaphors when it suited his purpose, although it must be said that some of his efforts are rather unhappy.[52] Certainly the lengthy metaphor with which the *Introduction* opens has, despite Bentham's warning, caused considerable confusion and has been taken as if he thought he was presenting a scientifically verifiable and specified proposition.

In the second place, in the sequel to the opening passage Bentham explicitly stated that the principle of utility does not admit of any direct proof, which, strictly speaking, precludes the possibility of its being demonstrated by an induction based on psychological hedonism. The absence of a direct proof, however, would not preclude the possibility of what John Stuart Mill later called an 'indirect proof', and, in this sense, both Bentham and Mill thought there was a connection between psychological and moral hedonism.[53] As Henry Sidgwick pointed out:

> . . . no cogent inference is possible from the psychological generalization to the ethical principle: but the mind has a natural tendency to pass from the one position to the other: if the actual ultimate springs of our volition are always our own pleasures and pains, it seems *prima facie* reasonable to be moved by them in proportion to their pleasantness and painfulness, and therefore to choose the greatest pleasure or the least pain on the whole.[54]

Psychological hedonism points to, though it does not prove, ethical hedonism. Bentham did not adopt Hume's distinction between 'is' and 'ought' statements because he wanted to make an epistemological or logical point. Rather he used it to criticise those like Blackstone who confused the law as it was with the law as it ought to be, thereby creating the impression that whatever is, is right. That famous passage in Hume, which led to a long tradition culminating in logical positivism which holds that ethical statements cannot be verified, was, in fact, consciously used by Bentham for ethical purposes. He distinguished between historical and censorial jurisprudence, and firmly placed himself in the latter camp. It was his understanding that what Hume, in general, had succeeded in doing was to prove that all statements, whether of the 'is' or the 'ought' type, can only admit of degrees of probability. There is no certainty in human knowledge, neither in jurisprudence nor in the natural sciences.[55] However much Bentham may have acted as if he was absolutely certain of the theory he was advancing, in terms of his theory of human knowledge he did not believe that absolute certainty was possible. Moreover, although he compared the science of morals and legislation to the science of medicine, he stressed that, while no one would dispute the end of medicine, namely, the health of the body, the end of morals and legislation, the health of the body politic, is disputed by many. In like manner he held that, while nothing prevents the science of physics from being accepted, 'in the Law the case has always been even under the best dispensation hitherto experienced by mankind that the necessity of the times' have 'made many articles receivable that have had no connection with' the proper end of law.[56] Nor did he always maintain, although he did so very often, that the failure to recognise the proper end of law was due to ignorance or sinister interest. 'The more I reflected, the more I was convinced that whatever might be my own notions on the several topics of Politics and Religion, others might persist in diametrical opposition to those opinions from very honest principles.'[57] It was because he was aware of such difficulties that he could, on occasion, speak of the principle of utility as a 'postulatum' or an 'hypothesis' or even as a 'gratuitious proposition'. Characteristically such remarks, like his views on geometry, remained unpublished although they appear in contexts quite similar to the more confident statements he chose to publish.[58]

It would certainly be wrong to think that Bentham really thought the principle of utility was gratuitious in any strict sense. One of the reasons he had for his confidence in the validity of the principle was that it was held by so many others such as Helvetius, Beccaria and Priestley, although he was seldom satisfied with the degree of consistency with which his fellow adherents traced out the implications of the principle. Indeed, he saw this to be the great contribution he was making. He did not claim to have discovered the principle, but only to have attempted to work out in detail the proper method of nomenclature and classification which would permit the principle to be applied with the thoroughness necessary to insure that the greatest happiness of the greatest number would be obtained.[59] It is difficult, perhaps impossible, to know why the doubts he admitted in the manuscripts in general fail to come through in his public proclamations. It may be that he later inadvertently provided a clue when he complained of those who, knowing that there are reasonable doubts to a position they hold, nonetheless assert it as self-evident and, by doing so, hope to put down any opposition from the start.[60] The possibility exists, then, that precisely because Bentham knew that his principle had been and would be challenged, he presented it in a manner best designed, in his eyes, to turn aside criticism. What better way of doing so, in an age where mathematics and science were supreme, than to write with their authoritative tones and in their language? Had not even Blackstone written that the study of law was the 'most rational branch of learning', described it as a 'science', and called for the establishment of 'a solid scientifical method'?[61] In any case, what is certain is that the early manuscripts frequently testify to Bentham's efforts to find the right way in which to address his audience (and, indeed, to decide who his audience was) as he first strikes one posture (apologetic, for example) and then another (aggressive). It is evident, then, that he was aware that the principle of utility was not simply self-evident, particularly in the extreme hedonic form in which he held it. It is also clear that he did not use such terms as 'axiom' in any consistent or precise sense (and this despite his own insistence on the need for consistency and precision), and that on one occasion he defined an 'axiom' in morals as 'a practice you *suppose* universally observed by others', which is, to say the least, a very ambiguous definition.[62]

Two further objections are frequently raised against Bentham's discussion of the principle of utility, namely, that he did not demonstrate that men are only motivated by pleasure and pain; and that, at best, psychological hedonism only points to an egoistic ethic, i.e. that each person ought to seek his own greatest happiness, and not to utilitarianism, i.e. that each person ought to seek the greatest happiness of the greatest number. The first objection is unanswerable. Bentham borrowed the notion of psychological hedonism from David Hartley,[63] and he never really tried to show how that theory might be supported with empirical evidence. It must be said that, as Bentham knew, other ethical theorists, including Aristotle, had maintained that there was a natural inclination to happiness; and had he known, he might have cited the fact that Kant admitted that men have a 'universal inclination to happiness'.[64] But whether happiness is measured only in terms of pleasure and the absence of pain is quite another matter. On his own terms, Bentham ought to have appealed to the feelings of mankind for evidence. Each person should ask himself whether or not he, in fact, is determined by the desire to gain pleasure or avoid pain, whether it be his own happiness or the greatest happiness of the greatest number. Now it does not appear that mankind makes any such admission. It is easy to point to instances where men claim to act on the basis of motives which are not only different from but opposed to any hedonic calculation. In terms of their feelings, they do not seem to confirm the hypothesis of psychological hedonism. Bentham apparently recognised this difficulty and, in response, he came close to saying that when an individual claims he is motivated, for example, by glory or duty, and that motivation has nothing to do with pleasure or pain, then he is deluded. What he really means is that glory or duty are particular forms of pleasure, although he does not like to admit it. But to argue in this way would seem to transform the question of psychological hedonism from a matter of fact to a matter of definition. Thus Bentham seems to maintain that, by definition, anything that motivates a person is either a pleasure or a pain. Bentham himself had been sharply critical of Locke for reducing ethics to a matter of definition in a foolish quest for certainty.[65] Yet it is clear that what is objectionable in ethics is much more so in an empirical science such as psychology.

Bentham would have been on safer ground had he argued that psychological hedonism describes a general rule or tendency in human behaviour. It is at least arguable that most men in most situations are motivated by considerations of pleasure and pain. Such an argument about the probable tendencies of human action would have been compatible with Bentham's general view of evidence which held that only probable, not certain, knowledge was accessible to man, whether in the natural or the moral sciences. But even if he had taken this line of argument, he still would have been left with a serious difficulty, and that is that, particularly in politics, the exceptions, be they heroic or demonic, to the hedonic theory of motivation often seem more important than the rule. This difficulty is related to the second objection mentioned above: does psychological hedonism point to an egoistic or a utilitarian ethic? Bentham seemed to have believed that the majority of men are chiefly moved by rather pedestrian considerations of their own personal happiness; they choose to act or to refrain from acting because of what they perceive the consequences might be for them, rather than because of the consequences for the greatest happiness of the greatest number. Bentham did not doubt that there were those who were guided by wider considerations of what he liked to call benevolence. After all, how else could he explain his own dedication to the public good which, on more than one occasion, caused him pain?[66] But such benevolence is exceptional. If egoism is, then, the psychological rule, while utilitarianism is the ethical norm, how would it be possible to obtain the greatest happiness of the greatest number? Would an individual cease pursuing his own greater happiness if he saw he would be causing greater unhappiness to others?

It has been argued, in this regard, that Bentham believed in the natural identification of interests: that as each individual pursues his own greatest personal happiness, the greatest happiness of the greatest number automatically results without anyone actually desiring it as such. Halévy summarised this view in the following way: 'Since it is recognised that the predominating motives in human nature are egoistic, and further that the human species lives and survives, it must be admitted that the various egoisms harmonise of their own accord and automatically bring about the good of the species.'[67] However, it is most unlikely that Bentham believed in the natural identification of interest. The whole purpose of his work was to teach the legislator to rear the fabric of felicity by means of reason and law, which certainly indicates that the legislator must work to provide the conditions most conducive to attaining the greatest happiness of the greatest number. Moreover, Bentham recognised that his reform proposals would require the sacrifice of particular interests to the interest of the community. 'The interest of the Public ought to be dear to every man', but this is not always the case in point of fact. However, the legislator does have a natural foundation from which to work, and that is the sentiment of sympathy which exists to some degree in most, perhaps all, men, and which increases as civilisation advances. Working with this social sentiment as well as with elements of self-regarding interest, the legislator must lead men to see that their own interest will ultimately be served if they seek the greatest happiness of the greatest number. Indeed, 'the proper and only useful business of Morality & Legislation is to establish and illustrate this connection between private & public Interest'.[68] To be sure, the legislator works primarily by employing pains which he inflicts via the penal sanction, and which are intended to prevent men from causing one another unhappiness:

> The case seems to be that in general there are more acts which men have need to be restrained from doing, than there are which they have need to be constrained to do. I mean more sorts of acts. Moreover let the sort of act be in the main ever so innocent, beneficial, or even necessary, it is only at certain seasons that it is so. The moments which give a man the opportunity of performing any positive service to the community are separated by long and frequent intervals: but mischief a man may do almost at any time. The great crimes such as murder, robbery, incendiarism, perjury and so forth are almost always committed by acts of the positive stamp. Mankind then, take the sum of their conduct throughout life have much greater need of a bridle than of a spur.[69]

But while the primary task of the legislator is to bring about the greatest happiness of the greatest number by placing restraints on man, there are also occasions when he acts, albeit indirectly, to educate the people to the benefits of acting benevolently, to show them how it is in their own interest to pursue the interest of others.[70]

In general, then, the transition from egoism to utilitarianism is a product of legislation broadly construed to include both penal sanctions and the education of public opinion. Desirable results might be accomplished with more or less difficulty for most men on most occasions. But the problem of exceptional individuals, including potentially the legislator himself, remains. What of those exceptional men whom Nietzsche was to call 'masters' and Bentham himself referred to as 'wolves'?[71] The legislator as legislator is beyond the reaches of the penal sanction, and Bentham recognised that there were men who were both above and below the moral sanction because, for one reason or another, they were not affected by the love of reputation.[72] Will those who have the sovereign political power automatically seek to promote the greatest happiness of the greatest number? Or will they, moved by their own egoistic interests, seek to promote their own greatest happiness at the expense of the greatest happiness of the greatest number? These and similar questions concerned Bentham throughout his long career as a reformer and ultimately contributed to turning him into a supporter of radical democracy, a transition which will be described and analysed in the following chapters of this study.

Notes Chapter I

1 UC 63, p. 11; UC 27, p. 173.
2 UC 27, p. 134; UC 99, p. 2.
3 *OLG*, p. 187 fn. d. and, in general, pp. 184–95; UC 27, p. 172. It would be tedious in the extreme to document how much Bentham was convinced that the failings of the common law were central to the difficulties confronting England. But in addition to *Of Laws in General*, see *A Comment on the Commentaries*, ed. C. W. Everett (Oxford, The Clarendon Press, 1928), particularly chs x, xiii–xx. Bentham may have underestimated the virtues of the common law but he was certainly not entirely wrong about its defects. See Leon Radzinowicz, *A History of English Criminal Law and its Administration from 1750*, 3 vols (New York, Macmillan, 1948, 1957), vol. 1, pp. 3–40 and *passim*.
4 *OLG*, p. 153.
5 ibid., p. 246. See also pp. 182–3 and UC 87, p. 12.
6 UC 79, pp. 1–137 and UC 95, pp. 1–118.
7 UC 27, pp. 103–4, 154 and UC 63, pp. 68, 71, 84–5. Bentham actually worked on a translation of and a preface for Bergmann's lectures on chemistry. See UC 156, especially pp. 1–5.
8 UC 63, p. 74.
9 *IPML*, p. 187 fn. a.
10 'Essay on Nomenclature and Classification', published in 1816 as an appendix to Bentham's papers on *Chrestomathia*. See *Works*, viii, pp. 63–128.

11 [Francis Jeffrey], *The Edinburgh Review*, vol. IV (April 1804), pp. 16–17.
12 UC 27, p. 103.
13 *OLG*, p. 251. See also UC 27, pp. 2–4, 45, 157–8; UC 69, pp. 149–50; UC 107, p. 4; UC 143, pp. 7–8; UC 169, pp. 1–5.
14 UC 69, p. 181.
15 UC 169, pp. 1–2. Also UC 69, pp. 127, 134.
16 UC 69, p. 214.
17 Elie Halévy, *The Growth of Philosophic Radicalism*, trans. Mary Morris (Boston, Mass., The Beacon Press, 1955), p. 34.
18 C. K. Ogden, *Bentham's Theory of Fictions* (London, Kegan Paul, Trench, Trubner, 1932), p. xxvi.
19 UC 69, p. 52. Also UC 46, p. 20.
20 Consider, for example, *Works*, I, pp. 236–8, 269, 291–5 (*A Fragment on Government*); *IPML*, pp. 102, 107, 187 fn. a, 190 fn. f, 271–2; *OLG*, pp. 43, 68–9 fn. n, 76 fn. a, 214–5 fn. j2, 243–5, 252, 278–9, 283 fn. k; UC 27, pp. 25–6, 88, 91, 139, 162; UC 46, p. 18; UC 69, pp. 70–1, 172–3, 205, 221; UC 90, p. 64; UC 140, pp. 7–8, 12.
21 C. W. Everett, *The Education of Jeremy Bentham* (New York, Columbia University Press, 1931), p. 197, Cf. Ogden, op. cit., p. xxx.
22 UC 159, pp. 164–7, quoted in Charles Blount, 'Bentham, Dumont and Mirabeau', *University of Birmingham Historical Journal*, vol. III (1952), p. 160. Sir Samuel Romilly wrote to Dumont in 1791 that 'Bentham leads the same kind of life as usual at Hendon; seeing nobody, reading nothing, and writing books which nobody reads'. *The Life of Sir Samuel Romilly, with a selection from His Correspondence*, 3rd edn., 2 vols (London, John Murray, 1842), vol. I, p. 318. For Bentham's own views on the difficulties of his new language consider UC 27, pp. 136, 139; UC 69, pp. 176–7; UC 140, p. 12. The essay to D'Alembert is in UC 169, pp. 52–66.
23 *Works*, I, pp. 292–3 fn. a (*A Fragment on Government*); *OLG*, pp. 294–5.
24 UC 27, pp. 88–94; UC 46, pp. 18–25; UC 96, pp. 19–20; UC 135, p. 50.
25 *OLG*, Appendix B, p. 251. Also UC 69, p. 152. See also *Works*, VIII, pp. 195–211 (*Ontology*).
26 *OLG*, p. 69.
27 *Works*, I, pp. 286–7, 291 (*A Fragment on Government*).
28 UC 69, pp. 60, 145–6, 156–7, 160–1, 177.
29 UC 69, p. 181. Psalm 106: 2: 'I said in my haste, All men are liars.'
30 This point will be discussed more fully in Chapter II.
31 UC 27, p. 123. Also p. 140.
32 *IPML*, p. 295.
33 ibid.
34 *Works*, I, p. 229 (*A Fragment on Government*); *IPML*, pp. 6, 295; *OLG*, pp. 45–6, 232–3.
35 *IPML*, pp. 11–12.
36 ibid., p. 13.
37 Halévy, op. cit., pp. 33–4.
38 *IPML*, pp. 25–6.
39 ibid., p. 12; *A Comment on the Commentaries*, pp. 154, 190–2.
40 On the first assumption see, for example, Jeremy Bentham, *Theory of Legislation*, trans. from the French of Etienne Dumont by Richard Hildreth (London, Trubner, 1876), pp. 102–9; UC 27, p. 70. On the second assumption see UC 27, p. 144; UC 63, pp. 74, 76; UC 72, pp. 187–210; UC 96, p. 121; UC 100, p. 114. A corollary of Bentham's consistent hedonism is

that no pain should be rejected as a punishment if it might prove to cause less pain than some other form of punishment. See W. L. and P. E. Twining, 'Bentham on Torture', *Bentham and Legal Theory*, ed. M. H. James, *Northern Ireland Legal Quarterly*, vol. XXIV (1973), pp. 39–90, which publishes and comments on UC 46, pp. 56–70.

41 UC 108, p. 111. See also UC 27, p. 127; UC 69, pp. 5–6, 73, 124, 132; and *A Comment on the Commentaries*, pp. 51–2 and *passim*.

42 *IPML*, pp. 9–10.

43 ibid., p. 13.

44 See, for example, ibid., p. 3.

45 UC 135, p. 36. For this and what follows see especially UC 135, pp. 4, 7, 19, 35–7, 39, 42, 44, 47–9, 50, 67. The manuscripts were prepared for the instruction of Bentham's brother, Sam, but Bentham seems to have thought in terms of publishing them. See Bentham to Samuel Bentham (20–26 August 1773), *The Correspondence of Jeremy Bentham: 1752–80*, ed. T. L. S. Sprigge, 2 vols (London, The Athlone Press, 1968), vol. I, pp. 158–9. Further references to these volumes will be cited as *Correspondence*.

46 UC 135, pp. 132, 397–9, 407.

47 *IPML*, p. 11.

48 Halévy, op. cit., p. 12.

49 David Hume, *A Treatise of Human Nature*, ed. L. A. Selby-Bigge (Oxford, The Clarendon Press, 1888), bk III, pt I, p. 469.

50 *Works*, I, pp. 268–9 fn. (*A Fragment on Government*); *Works*, V, p. 389 (*Humphrey's Real Property Code*); *Works*, VIII, p. 128 fn. (*Chrestomathia*).

51 *IPML*, p. 11.

52 Thus UC 27, p. 137 contrasts 'the complete froth of rhetorical declamation and poetic fiction' with 'the instructive milk of science'!

53 *IPML*, p. 13. J. S. Mill, 'Utilitarianism', *Essays on Ethics, Religion and Society* in the *Collected Works of John Stuart Mill*, vol. X (Toronto, The University of Toronto Press, 1969), pp. 234–9.

54 Henry Sidgwick, *The Methods of Ethics*, 7th edn (New York, Dover, 1966), p. 42.

55 UC 46, pp. 1–4; UC 27, p. 7.

56 UC 63, p. 78.

57 UC 27, p. 105.

58 UC 100, p. 114; UC 27, pp. 15, 103. David Baumgardt, *Bentham and the Ethics of Today* (New York, Octagon Books, 1966) remains an indispensable guide to understanding the evolution and nature of Bentham's ethical theory.

59 UC 27, pp. 99–100.

60 *Works*, VII, p. 451 (*Rationale of Judicial Evidence*). See also *OLG*, p. 303 fn. f.

61 *Commentaries on the Laws of England*, 4 vols, 15th edn (London, 1809), vol. I, pp. 3–4, 33.

62 UC 135, p. 5. See also UC 27, 20–2; UC 69, p. 198; UC 135, p. 14.

63 David Hartley, *Observations on Man, His Frame, His Duty, and His Expectations* (London, 1749).

64 Aristotle, *Nicomachean Ethics*, I, vii, 3–8; Immanuel Kant, *Foundations of the Metaphysics of Morals*, trans. Lewis White Beck (Indianapolis, Bobbs-Merrill, 1959), p. 15.

65 UC 27, p. 7.

66 UC 27, pp. 26, 46, 55, 112; UC 69, pp. 176–7.

67 Halévy, op. cit., p. 15. Also David Lyons, *In the Interest of the Governed* (Oxford, Clarendon Press, 1973), pp. 19–105.

68 UC 71, p. 21; UC 27, pp. 10, 13, 16, 102.

69 *OLG*, pp. 111–12 fn. o.

70 UC 87, pp. 18–19, 62; UC 97, p. 60.

71 Friedrich Nietzsche's discussion of 'masters' and 'slaves' may be found in many of his works, but see, in particular, *Beyond Good and Evil*, pt IX. Bentham writes of the morality of 'wolves' and 'sheep' in *Works*, v, p. 291 (*Defence of Economy against Burke*).

72 *OLG*, pp. 202–3; UC 98, p. 6.

Chapter II

Obstacles to Reform

In his old age Bentham recalled his early optimistic belief that the imperfections in government would easily be swept away when the 'correct and instructive encyclopaedical arrangement' he was developing was adopted. He saw himself as 'a great reformist: but never suspected that the people in power were against reform. I supposed they only wanted to know what was good in order to embrace it.'[1] He was to be disappointed:

> Instead of the universal sympathy, of which I had expected to see these graspings after improvement productive in those higher regions, universal antipathy – antipathy on the part of all parties – was the result: proofs of the fact came in upon me one after another; but sixty years had rolled over my head before I had attained to anything like a clear perception of the cause.[2]

Only after those sixty years of disappointment did he realise that 'man, from the very constitution of his nature, prefers his own happiness to that of all other sensitive beings put together'.[3] Only after realising the pre-eminence of the self-preference principle was he able to understand why his naïve optimism had been so severely disappointed:

> If self-preference has place in every human breast, then, if rulers are men, so must it have in every ruling breast. Government has, accordingly, under every form comprehending laws and institutions, had for its object the greatest happiness, not of those over whom, but of those by whom, it has been exercised; the interests not of the many, but of the few, or even of the one, has been the prevalent interest; and to that interest all others have been, at all times sacrificed.[4]

His reform proposals would have improved the lot of the greater number but, at the same time, they would have threatened the interests of the rulers who, perceiving this, were compelled by their natural self-preference to oppose his suggestions and turn their antipathy against him.

It is difficult to know why Bentham created this legend of the innocent young reformer, totally unaware that there might be objections and opposition to his proposals, particularly from those in power. It is true that in his later years he advocated radical democracy because he was convinced that only in such a regime would the interests of the governors also be the interests of the governed, while in his youth (and for a very long time) he was hopeful of achieving reform within the general structure of English government. It is true that, in his later writings, there is much more emphasis on the power of the self-preference principle among ruling groups. But the early manuscripts make it clear that he knew that both the principle of utility and the specific changes he was proposing in the light of it would meet with considerable opposition. Indeed, at one point he proposed writing an *Essay on the Obstacles to the Advancement of the Science* of jurisprudence. He drew up a chart indicating the various obstacles which would have to be overcome, and wrote a fair number of pages on the subject. There would be obstacles as a result of prejudice and interest. Prejudicial opposition would be found among professional men (in particular, legislators and divines), men of old age, and the people at large. Obstacles would also come from the interests of professionals (again lawyers and divines and, in addition, other authors and booksellers whose work would be rendered obsolete by Bentham's writings!), legislators, and adherents to political parties.[5]

Although Bentham at times wrote optimistically about the universal spread of learning, he recognised that there would be resistance to change from the common people. They tended to be complacent about the evils which they suffered, and blamed them on the nature of things. They did not realise that the real cause of their sufferings, in fact, was the English system of law. In general, they blindly accepted the English Constitution as excellent, believing without question that everything was as it ought to be. The result was that they often opposed reforms designed to benefit them, fearful, among other things, that their ancient liberties might be endangered by change.[6] Bentham was convinced that the people would look with hostility at his suggestions for greater sexual and religious freedom, so much so that this was one of the reasons he suppressed those suggestions, in the main, until 1818. Certainly he was right in presuming that there was little to be gained and much to be lost in trying to show, for example, that homosexuality was not only wrongly punished but that it was a positive good, or that incest ought not to be a crime.[7] In any case, Bentham did not much concern himself about how he might convince the people at large of the worth of his proposals: 'The herd of the people must for a long time perhaps forever be sway'd chiefly by authority: but of those who by their authority are in a way to lead them there are enough whose circumstances admitt of their being sway'd by reason.'[8] Bentham felt that his undertaking was far too difficult to be comprehended by men in general and, accordingly, he addressed himself to legislators, actual or potential, who might be capable of learning from him. It would be their responsibility to introduce and win support for his reform proposals. To be sure, Bentham was ready to give them advice as to how they might best proceed, and it is worth noting that the advice was generally of a cautious kind. Although he held that any sovereign who was truly interested in reform could overcome popular prejudice, he warned against running too hard against popular feelings. To do so would be unwise since it would risk creating hostility toward beneficial reforms. It would also be wrong. The feelings of the people, even if rooted in prejudice and false morality, deserve to be consulted. Not to do so would cause them pain, and that pain would detract from the existing greatest happiness. Reforms should only be implemented if there was some certainty that the actual gain in happiness resulting from the reforms was significantly greater than the pain caused by altering existing practices. In general, Bentham sought to outline means of subtly drawing the people along to reform, and his suggestions include some of his most impressive as well as some of his most crotchety ideas.[9]

It would be the task of the legislator, then, to convince the people of the utility of reform. But it was Bentham's task to convince the legislator, and the difficulty of convincing legislators to embrace reform obviously perplexed him. In regard to England, he accepted the view that the sovereign power rested in the King in Parliament. Although he later recalled that in his early years he had been an enthusiastic admirer of George III, his memoirs, as we have already seen, are notoriously untrustworthy. There is little evidence in the early manuscripts and letters to indicate how he then felt the King might take to reform.[10] But given Bentham's feelings about the Church of England, and the role of the bishops in the House of Lords, it is easy to see how he felt the chances for reform would be so far as they depended on the co-operation of the Lords. Moreover, as has already been indicated, he felt that the Church had used its morally corrupting and intellectually enervating education in such a way as to ruin the minds and the spirits of a majority of the members of the House of Commons.[11] If nothing else stood in the way of reform, then the Church surely did. But the Church did not stand alone. The divines had active allies in the members of what Bentham called the lawyers' tribe. Lawyers were more likely than most people to be unduly enamoured by the alleged excellences of the English Constitution, and hence to be prejudicially blinded to the real interests of the people. But it was not the prejudice of the lawyers which alone worried Bentham. Rather it was the vested interest which the lawyers had in preserving, intact, the English system of law. The confusions and complexities of common law jurisprudence meant money to them. Even the simplest case required their expert advice, since there was no way of knowing what the relevant legal precedents were except by consulting them. Complicated procedural requirements and 'hearings' which never really took place not only dragged out judicial contests but greatly increased the fees of the lawyers. The defects of the system were 'the patrimony of the profession'. A lawyer able to make £8,000 to £10,000 per year out of the defects of the system could hardly be expected to work for reforms which would jeopardise his interest.[12] The lawyers were aided and abetted in their exploitation of the public by their fellow professionals, the judges, who also profited financially from the fee-paying system and who, in addition, were jealous of the political power they had effectively usurped from the legislature under the guise of the common law. Churchmen, lawyers, judges – alone and together they infected the English Constitution with the 'Spirit of Civil Tyranny' and the 'Spirit of Dogmatic Theology'.[13]

> Those among whom a great interest is shared, being few may form themselves into a body and act in concert: if they are already embodied, their power is still more formidable.
>
> If the stronger interest taking extent into consideration were universally prevalent, every thing would be as it should be. [T]here would be no bad government; men would every where be as happy as good government could make them.[14]

Things were much closer to the former case than to the latter in England. Bentham was convinced that the churchmen, lawyers and judges had considerable influence, and that they were well aware that it was in their interest to act in concert to block reform. Though they might be a minority in Parliament, as the lawyers certainly were in the Commons, the strength of their selfish interest made them the active force within the system. The rest of the legislators tended to be indolent. Many of them were heirs to wealth and had no motive to cause them to develop their abilities or to move them to pursue the public good, particularly when it would mean difficult labour and the risk of hostility from members of their own class. Where there is no motive, there is no activity. Was it any wonder, then, that Bentham could comment that if he produced any ideas worth using, his countrymen might think of turning them to account perhaps one hundred years after his death?[15] If Bentham was optimistic about the possibilities for reform in his youth, it was certainly not naïve optimism of the kind he depicted in his late recollections.

Now the perplexing question is, if Bentham was well aware of deeply rooted obstacles to reform in his early years, why did he fail to take into consideration the possible need for constitutional reform as a necessary prelude to penal reformation? Constitutional debate abounded during his formative years as the Whig consensus established in 1689, and consolidated during the opening decades of the eighteenth century, began to show signs of falling apart. Bentham, though only fifteen years old, was a senior commoner at Oxford in 1753 when John Wilkes was brought to trial, and, according to an entry in Jeremiah Bentham's diary, Bentham attended the trial.[16] By 1769, when Wilkes returned from his self-imposed exile in France, Bentham was living in chambers and busily tracing out the implications of the principle of utility. Wilkes's actions had raised serious constitutional questions: 'He brought Parliament into great disrepute. He demonstrated by his actions its unrepresentative nature; its dependence on the Crown; its corruption and prejudice – facts known for decades, but never so amply demonstrated; nor had the danger to personal liberty, so inherent in such a system, been so clearly proved.'[17] The same issues were also raised by the growing restlessness of the American colonies during the same period and after. Debates about the representative or unrepresentative character of Parliament, the relative powers of King and Commons, as well as the nature of the relationship between the colonies and the mother country flourished. Major John Cartwright, later Bentham's ally in the fight for radical reform, who had already struck his colours in 1774 with a pamphlet proclaiming *American Independence: The Interest and Glory of Great Britain*, published *Take Your Choice!* in 1776. This pamphlet called for annual parliaments and equal representation in England as the only alternative to the existing despotism.[18] Richard Price expressed similar sentiments in *Observations on the Nature of Civil Liberty*.[19] As the Government under Lord North floundered through the war with the colonies, hostility toward the King increased and by 1780 reached such a pitch that the House of Commons itself, sitting in Committee, passed the Dunning Resolution declaring 'that the influence of the Crown has increased, is increasing, and ought to be diminished'.[20] Through all of these events, Bentham remained remarkably silent, although he did express his dismay over Wilkes's activity, condemning him as a perfectly abhorrent person, and he briefly attacked the natural rights teaching of the American Declaration of Independence.[21] Given the importance of the issues raised during the period, and their obvious bearing on the greatest happiness of the greatest number, it is very odd, indeed, that this prolific writer and ardent reformer had so little to say. In later years he was to maintain that:

On the texture of the *constitutional* branch of law, will depend that of

> every other. For on this branch of law depends, in all its branches, the *relative and appropriate aptitude* of those functionaries, on whose will depends, at all times, the texture of every other branch of law. If, in the framing of this branch of law, the greatest happiness of the greatest number is taken for the end in view, and that object pursued with corresponding success, so will it be in the framing of those other branches: if not, not.[22]

Yet well into his middle age he generally avoided constitutional questions, although at times he showed an awareness that his silence was curious. Thus, in 1781, he wrote apologetically to Lord Shelburne about his failure to bestow attention 'upon the constitutional branch of law', offering as his excuse the fact that it was his 'way . . . first to consider what is *possible*, next what is *eligible* and lastly what is *established*'.[23] It was, as he seems to have realised, a limp excuse, yet similar somewhat embarrassed apologies appear in variant forms in the *Fragment on Government*, the *Introduction to the Principles of Morals and Legislation* and the manuscript for *Of Laws in General*.[24] Not to put too fine an edge on it, he was almost entirely concerned with penal laws designed to keep people from harming one another, and not all with constitutional law which might keep the government from harming the people or lead it to help them in ways other than mere crime prevention.

Despite Bentham's undeniable failure to make any sustained analysis of constitutional questions during the years from 1769 to 1789, there are some interesting occasional comments which help one to understand his position. Not surprisingly, in one committed to a new dictionary or grammar for morals and legislation, the attention he does give to constitutional questions is largely given to the meaning of words. Constitutional terminology was as muddled as legal terminology proper. There was a great need for clarifying such words as 'representative'. He speculated that 'delegate' might be a better description of the Members of Parliament since one can and does speak of the King and Lords as 'representatives' of the people though it would surely be wrong to describe them as 'delegates'. Yet, in another place, he rejected the notion of 'virtual representation', since it was not representation in any meaningful sense of the word.[25] As these examples suggest, Bentham was not clear in his own mind about such matters for if the King might be described as a representative of the people it would surely be as a virtual representative.

In other fragmentary discussions, Bentham claimed to be attempting the 'novel task' of precisely defining the nature of executive, legislative and judicial power.[26] He maintained that the sum total of power in any government, irrespective of form, is the same but he also held that 'a tyranny of a man . . ., though less discernible, yet when once discerned is more formidable and at any rate more baneful than a tyranny of the laws'.[27] He emphatically rejected the notion of Blackstone and Montesquieu that the three powers of government were separate in the English Constitution. Sovereignty in England rests 'in the King, Lords, and Commons in Parliament assembled' and that sovereignty can only be exercised through the co-operation of the three branches.[28] Bentham's attempt to get behind the fictions of constitutional theory caused him to criticise those who placed their hope on 'the accidental personal qualifications of the individual' holding a given office, and to mock those who believed that because a person was in a class called 'Aristocratic', he would have the virtue and merit associated with the name. One must examine an actual position and see what motives exist to compel the holder of any office to exercise that office in an appropriate manner, and not trust in mere words. It must be in the interest of an individual to do his duty, for to presume that anyone will otherwise do what he ought to do is naïve.[29] In these and other ways, Bentham anticipated positions which he would work out in considerable detail in later years. Moreover, he was also critical of all systems of law since, 'even under the best dispensation', they have contained many elements unconnected with the greatest happiness of the greatest number. Indeed, they were established without any conscious attention being paid to the only proper end of government:

> So as to the form of Constitution – they who established Monarchy or Aristocracy never set themselves to inquire whether Monarchy or Aristocracy was the best government for the people – Monarchy or Aristocracy was at all events to be upholden – The Laws that were to be made were to be no other than such as were calculated to uphold it – That end, which if it had been recognized for that to which Laws relative to this title as well as to every other, were to be fashioned, might if freely consulted, have dictated Laws of a very different nature – The business was therefore to keep it as much as possible out of view.[30]

If constitutional theorists had examined the English Constitution in the light of the principle of utility they would have condemned practices which harm the people. But they had not done so. 'The main and almost only ends men had in view in administering what was called Justice, was the advancement of what was called piety and what was called Royalty. What was not done to the honour of God was done to the profit of the King. The King was every thing: the people nothing.'[31] Or again:'The standing principle of the good old English common law is that the King is every thing: and that if the welfare of the people is worth attending to it is because they are his property.'[32] While improvements had been made in the treatment of the people since the early days of monarchy, none the less many abuses persisted. The English Constitution was not wholly designed to secure the greatest happiness of the greatest number.

These are strange sentiments coming from one who recalled late in life that he had been an unabashed royalist and supporter of King George III and the aristocracy in his early years. Perhaps he was, prior to 1775–6, but in those years he was scribbling away on the virtues of legislative supremacy within the English Constitution. He felt that the House of Commons was, or rather ought to be, the active element in government, and believed that only where there was active interest could one hope to obtain utilitarian ends.[33] He even speculated about the contribution to be made to the happiness of the people by extending the franchise. Characteristically his remarks are buried in the midst of a discussion of injuries inflicted *in alienam personam*, i.e. when in punishing a guilty party one inflicts an injury on another person who is not guilty. In 1771 the majority of the electors of the borough of New Shoreham had been disenfranchised for open election corruption. The remaining electors had been thrown into an enlarged election district where the franchise was given to forty-shilling freeholders. Bentham felt that this inflicted punishment on the uncorrupted voters by diminishing the relative weight of their vote. And he added:

> But in whatever light it may appear, considered with reference to the particular persons subjected to that trifling disadvantage, as a measure of reformation it can not but be too highly praised. It stands as the pattern and ground work of a great plan of constitutional improvement. It distributes & throws into more hands the great privilege of election, the only branch of power which a great body of the people can find it for their advantage to possess.[34]

While this is hardly radicalism, whether measured by the views of men like Cartwright and Price in these years or by the views Bentham himself was later to hold, nevertheless it is indicative of his awareness of the need for constitutional change. Yet he not only was content with a very gradual alteration of the franchise, but he did not particularly see that it was his task to campaign actively for such moderate change.

In respect to his silence, it must be noted that Bentham was quite cautious, until late in life, about putting into print his views on delicate or controversial subjects. Despite the depth of his hostility toward the Church of England, he not only generally muted his views but he even included a Church of England chaplain in his proposed Panopticon prison. Constitutional issues obviously struck him as similarly dangerous matters for discussion and he feared that, if he were to discuss them, it might cost him the support of those he thought might assist him in working for reform of the penal law. The latter reforms would be easier to obtain and they would have a more direct impact on the happiness of most people.[35] He felt that to support either the Whigs or the Tories might jeopardise the chances for success, since party jealousy would create enemies where none had previously existed. Indeed, there would be jealousy even within the party he might choose to support, for party men are ever suspicious of the ideas brought forth by others, and suspicious jealousy increases with the merits of the proposals.[36] Thus he consistently presented himself as a 'no party' man, a stratagem reinforced by the fact that he did believe that many of his proposals for reform transcended not merely party, but even national boundaries. The laws of physics are everywhere the same; so too should be the laws of politics. His reforms would be good for all nations, whether democratic, aristocratic or monarchic. This belief had a certain plausibility precisely to the extent that Bentham focused on the day-to-day workings of penal laws for theft, arson, murder, embezzlement and the like; and stressed the advantages to be gained from a uniform penal code, system of procedure and judicial organisation. Just as obviously, it became dubious to the extent that he turned to such crimes as 'state libels' and one finds him straining to convince a monarch that it would be in his own interest to permit a free press and not to punish libellous statements about the regime.[37]

But Bentham seldom found it necessary in his early years to enter into such controversial discussions. He was convinced that there was little any government could do positively to promote the happiness of its people. While government could prevent happiness, for example, by banning the theatre, it could not cause the people to seek given forms of pleasure. The individual alone could decide what particular activities would bring him pleasure. In general, all government could do was to provide the general conditions within which the individual would be secure in the pursuit of happiness; and see to it that the individual did not, in that pursuit, jeopardise the happiness of the greatest number.[38] Furthermore, Bentham did not see any sufficient reason why, in any form of government, it should be against the interest of the rulers to see the security of the people increased. The highwayman who intimidated the lowliest subject was as much, or perhaps a greater, threat to the highest, and Bentham believed that similar coincidences of interest for the people as a whole could be shown to be true for many other criminal offences.

There is one last factor to be considered in estimating Bentham's relative silence about constitutional questions in his early years. Although he saw himself as proposing legislation for any nation, he was particularly interested in reform within England. While he recognised that there were aspects of the English system which were not conducive to the greatest happiness of the greatest number, it is clear that, on balance, he thought the system was meritorious. In general an atmosphere of freedom prevailed which meant that conditions were conducive to reform. Men like Cartwright and Price could speak out because restrictions on freedom of publication were the exception rather than the rule. Public opinion did count, although Bentham thought there were ways, such as the establishment of an 'Office of Intelligence' to gather letters from persons whose interests were affected by laws, which could make public opinion operate more efficiently.[39] It was best in Bentham's eyes that public opinion should operate in such regular channels. He genuinely deplored the mob. He described those who set up a flag proclaiming 'Wilkes and Liberty' as 'mad' and he expressed similar sentiments during the Gordon riots in 1780.[40] The very language of constitutional debate lent itself too readily to dangerous tendencies:

> In constitutional topics like these, and under popular governments more especially, the judgments of men are in continual danger of being disturbed by the influence of their passions: nor is it to be wondered at if a consciousness of the inferences that may be drawn from the significations assigned to particular words should on such occasions dispose them to regard the most phlegmatic and impartial discussions with an eye of jealousy.[41]

Constitutional questions were abstract and remote from the normal interests of the common man whose primary concerns, after all, must be with his family and his fortune. If, as seems the case, Bentham held to the view that truth would win out in the market place, it was not because he had great confidence in the people, but because he counted on a few men who would be responsive to popular needs as articulated by thinkers like himself. Even though he was insistent that the feelings of the people must be taken into consideration, his very concept of the legislative function suggest that change would come from above and not from below.

But the problem still remains, and that is how did Bentham believe the reformation of the law could be brought about, given the fact that he was aware of the obstacles standing in the way of reform? Charles Tarlton is on the right track in describing what he calls the 'overlooked strategy' of Bentham's *Fragment on Government:*

> Many of the most generally abstract and aloof political treatises (in addition to the more frankly operational) reflect a willingness 'strategically' to attach the good of the people to the ambitions of the

> ruling minority. By a process akin in many ways to alchemy, the writer then seeks to show the ruler that in the long run it is his own best interests that are served by tempering his personal desires in deference to the needs of those whom he rules. The assumption has seemed to be that among men of the world the maintenance of power is a question of hard-headed realities, and that lapses of extreme pride, vanity, or undue attachment to empty symbols and vain rhetoric are easily overcome by an astute and timely directing of attention back to the real demands of order, peace, prosperity, and security. All that even the most thoroughly selfish ruler need be shown, the argument suggests, is that the most effective (and probably the cheapest) guarantee of his own tenure is achieved through the liberalising modifications of certain laws, institutions, practices. None but a fool, then, would fail to act, and thus, indirectly, reform is successfully urged. The rule, then, is a simple one: the greatest danger to the exercise of power is unnecessary irritation of those over whom it is exercised.[42]

Although Tarlton misjudges how difficult Bentham thought the task of convincing the rulers would be, nevertheless something like this strategy did play a role in Bentham's attempt to win favour for his reform proposals. He felt that men who seek power were more apt to calculate and, hence, were more amenable to reasonable arguments, including appeals to their self-interest.[43] But it was not simply appeals to crass self-interest, through lightly veiled threats of danger, which Bentham chose to use. He also believed that there were those in the ruling class who could be won over to the cause of reform by appealing to their sense of honour or the desire for glory or the desire to contribute to the wellbeing of the people.

This is a point which deserves more attention than it has received in Bentham scholarship. Even in his late radical period Bentham insisted that some men acted out of what he called effective benevolence, a genuine concern for their fellow men. It is often argued that his doctrine of egoistic motivation vitiates any element of unselfishness:

> Is not so-called unselfishness simply a means to an end? a price which the individual pays in order to secure the good will, and the good services, of his neighbours? Bentham did not believe in *genuine* self-sacrifice, self-sacrifice devoid of a desire to gain prestige or power or some other selfish gratification: to him man is and remains a born egoist – an egoist not only in his deeds, but even in his very thoughts.[44]

Thus the notion prevails that Bentham really only saw men as acting out of narrow considerations of self-interest. Benevolence or honour or glory, power entirely out of the account, are simply reducible to crass egoistic considerations. Indeed, only the most vulgar considerations move men. Since Bentham once remarked that 'money is the instrument measuring the quantity of pain or pleasure', commentators have held that 'this conviction that money measures psychic experiences is carried very far by Bentham. Every pain, he claims, is capable of measurement, because every pain is capable of compensation.'[45] Because this estimate of Bentham is so widespread, it is interesting to discover him, in his early years, criticising those who wish to extirpate duelling precisely because they ignore the fact that there are injuries which cannot be compensated for by money. Duelling ought to be permitted because it provides a suitable means of compensating injuries to honour in a way money never could.[46]

Whatever might be true of Bentham's later years, in the early years he was not a crude reductionist in psychology. Bentham was first and foremost a reformer, and his interest in psychology only stemmed from his interest in reform. Not only did he see no need to reduce every motive to the lowest egoistic denominator but he felt that it was inimical to reform to do so: 'Machiavel supposes his statesman a villain and then teaches him how he may fulfill his purposes: I suppose my statesman a patriot and a philantropist or what comes to the same thing a man of understanding.'[47] Men of understanding know the value of the honour or glory to be won by being benefactors of mankind. Moreover, Bentham held that the satisfaction of such desires brings pleasures in itself, entirely aside from any other considerations. To be sure, the pleasure gained from acting benevolently is my pleasure, but it is a pleasure which comes and can only come from helping others, and it may come even if those others do not express their gratitude. Bentham was quite insistent in rejecting the suggestion that a person who acts benevolently must do so out of some ulterior consideration. He deplored the 'vulgar' error 'that nothing has its value with mankind but money: power, rank, consideration, nothing that you can name', and he added sarcastically, 'ignorance like this ought to be left to English lawyers, who build upon it their law of verbal scandal, their law of evidence, and so many others of their laws – judging of other men by themselves, and not knowing how to do justice, even to themselves'.[48] Indeed, it seems likely that this view of English lawyers had been brought home to Bentham early on because of his own intimate relationship with one of the lawyers' tribe, his own father. As he wrote to his brother, Sam, in 1775, about their father: 'He certainly does love you and me next to his money I was going to say however very nearly if not altogether equal to his wife.'[49] And again, in 1777, referring to his father under the not entirely affectionate code name 'Q.S.P.,' which stood for Jeremiah's Queens Square Place residence:

> Q.S.P. had been at his favourite amusement; pulling to pieces poor Sr. J. Hawkins without mercy: drawing his own picture, and putting Sr. John's name to it. 'He was the greatest "*egotist*" that ever lived'– (meaning by *egotist* all the while not what other people mean by it, vain, but '*selfish*' – But egotist you know has Latin in it) 'He drew every thing to himself' – 'He never did a man a favour in his life, but *self* was at the bottom of it – ' etc. etc. being just what I had heard *in terminis* a hundred times over from the same mouth.[50]

Not very flattering words to describe one's father, but they none the less indicate that Bentham did not believe that money was the measure of all things nor that all action could be described in terms of crude selfishness. It was precisely because he felt that English lawyers were all too motivated by the love of money that he disliked them so intensely and saw them as a chief obstacle to reforms which would cost them dearly. But lawyers were not the whole of the establishment. Were there not some within the establishment who might be moved by that purest and most social motive of benevolence, reinforced and cultivated by the love of reputation?[51] Certainly Bentham himself was so moved in his attempt to establish a new science of morals and legislation, and he hoped that he would find kindred spirits among those in power. He thought of writing to Edmund Burke to interest him in particular reforms,[52] and he tried, ultimately with success, to bring himself to the attention of Lord Shelburne.[53] It was clearly through the agency of such men that Bentham hoped to win a hearing for his reform proposals.

Bentham, then, seems to have considered using both threats of the kind described by Tarlton, and appeals to benevolence and honour or the love of reputation. He seems to have hoped that, perhaps, the House of Commons might respond if it realised that, under the English Constitution, it was supposed to be supreme in enacting legislation but that, in fact, its power had been usurped by the judiciary. Perhaps pride, perhaps jealousy among the Members of Parliament would stir them to reform the penal law.[54] In any case, as the manuscripts in particular make clear, Bentham considered appealing to a range of motives and employing a diversity of strategies in order to gain support. But it also seems the case that he was not quite clear as to which would be the most effective approach and this uncertainty may, in part, account for his general failure to complete so many projects. As his friend, George Wilson, scolded: 'But your history, since I have known you, has been to be always running from a good scheme to a better. In the meantime, life passes away and nothing is completed.'[55] As the years went on, Bentham appears to have become increasingly disillusioned about the prospects of reform in England. Though England, with her freedom, was the best of places for reform ideas to develop, it was among the least likely places for the ideas to take hold.[56] The very virtues of the English Constitution made men complacent about the need for reform, and Bentham began to look abroad, and especially to Russia, where Catherine the Great was not only actively engaged in reform but had actually embraced the principle of the greatest happiness of the greatest number. Samuel Bentham had left for Russia in 1779. Arriving there in the spring of 1780, he gradually developed contacts with the Court and by 1783 had entered the service of Catherine, 'with the rank of lieutenant-colonel, and accompanied Prince Potemkin to Krichev in White Russia, to assist him in his grandiose schemes for the development of the southern steppes'.[57] Bentham joined Sam in 1786 with the expectation that perhaps in Russia he might find a favourable response to his codification proposals. Whatever his hopes, not much was accomplished, although he stayed in Russia for two years. As J. H. Burns has written: 'Catherine never saw either the Code or its author. Bentham remained secluded in western Russia, translating his work into French; and when the empress visited the district he stayed – stubbornly diffident – in his cottage.'[58]

Bentham returned to England in 1788 and, shortly after his return, came the first stirrings of the French Revolution. Bentham quickly saw a new opportunity for advancing his reform proposals. By November 1788 he was drafting pamphlets on French affairs, writing 'in his own highly individual French, polemics against the *Parlement* of Paris or the *noblesse* of Brittany', which, as Burns has noted, 'was to carry not so much coals as clinker to Newcastle'.[59]

> At the same time, the occasion drew Bentham into reflections of more lasting importance. He set out to answer the questions about the organization of the States General submitted to the reconvened Assembly of the Notables. Part of this discussion became virtually what Bentham himself called it a few months later – 'an essay on Representation'. This asserts quite sweepingly democratic principles derived from utilitarian assumptions, and it has played a controversial part in interpretations of the development of Bentham's political thought.[60]

There is no question about the democratic principles developed in the 'essay' as well as in other manuscripts written between 1788-91. Bentham argued, for example, that each person has 'an equal right' to 'all the happiness that he is capable of'. Because it is difficult to determine the relative degree of happiness different individuals are likely to receive from a given activity, it is necessary, particularly in political contexts, to presume that the degree is the same for everyone. But if happiness is to be gained from the activity of exercising the franchise, then a strong presumption exists for establishing equal voting rights so as best to distribute this form of happiness to the public. While exclusions from equal voting rights might be made, for example, in the case of minors or the insane, they must be made on the basis of 'clearly pronounced and sensible indices'.[61] The burden of proof for excluding any one person or any class of persons falls on those who are in favour of the exclusion.

The controversy over the 'essay on Representation' and related writings is largely over whether or not Bentham had in these years become a firmly committed democrat. Bentham himself felt that he did not really embrace democracy until 1809, and Halévy, in agreeing with him, maintained that the 1788–91 manuscripts represented only a highly speculative attempt on Bentham's part to entertain, as he often did, possible interpretations which might be given in the light of the principle of utility.[62] On the other hand, Mary Mack has argued that Bentham was fully committed to democratic reform by 1789, and that his failure to push ahead with concrete reform proposals was merely a 'Fabian retreat', forced upon him by the turn of events in France and the increasing hostility toward the French by the English Government and the people alike.[63]

What is certain is that Bentham's speculations were to be outstripped by events. By 1791 he began to be disillusioned by the increasingly radical turn the Revolution was taking in France. He had condemned the anarchic implications of the American Declaration of Independence in 1776, but initially he was willing to tolerate the French Declaration of Rights and even to use its language. But increasingly he saw that the French were taking such notions as equal rights quite seriously. Men were being put to death and property threatened in the name of doctrines which he felt to be chimerical. By 1795 he was composing a work to be called *Pestulance Unmasked!* (which was later published as *Anarchical Fallacies*), a ringing condemnation of the French Declaration of the Rights of Man and the actions perpetrated in its name. As J. H. Burns has remarked, to describe Bentham's flight from democratic parliamentary reforms as a 'Fabian retreat' is 'to call Dunkirk a tactical withdrawal'.[64] In fact, for almost two decades after 1791, Bentham not only wrote nothing on behalf of parliamentary reform but he wrote almost nothing about politics proper. He buried himself in his attempt to establish a model Panopticon prison, writing thousands upon thousands of pages describing, explaining and defending 'this quintessentially Benthamic project';[65] and turning out as many, if not more, pages on the subject of judicial evidence. There was, however, one other topic of importance which caught his interest in those years of retreat, and that was the subject of economics; and it is in his writings on economics that one finds him changing from viewing government as an essentially negative, restraining force, toward viewing government as making positive contributions to the greatest happiness of the greatest number.

Notes Chapter II

1 *Works*, x, pp. 80, 66.
2 ibid., p. 80.
3 ibid.
4 ibid., p. 81.
5 UC 169, p. 1; UC 27, p. 10; UC 97, p. 1.
6 UC 27, pp. 8, 139, 161; UC 63, p. 11.
7 UC 72, pp. 187–210. See also, the Introduction to the present study and my essay, 'Morality and Belief: The Origin and Purpose of Bentham's Writings on Religion', *The Mill News Letter*, vi (Spring 1971), pp. 3–15.
8 UC 27, p. 135.
9 UC 71, p. 48. In general, see the materials on 'indirect legislation' in UC 88, pp. 1–194 and Bentham's *Theory of Legislation*, pp. 358–472.
10 But see UC 27, pp. 46, 102, 161; UC 169, p. 79.
11 UC 96, pp. 316–23. See my 'Morality and Belief', op. cit., p. 5.
12 UC 27, pp. 96, 123.
13 UC 63, p. 68. Also UC 27, p. 123 and UC 63, p. 70.
14 UC 69, p. 168.
15 UC 27, pp. 124, 152. Also UC 27, p. 105; UC 69, p. 130; UC 97, pp. 26, 29, 76–7; *Works*, i, p. 295 (*A Fragment on Government*).
16 *Works*, x, p. 45.
17 J. H. Plumb, *England in the Eighteenth Century* (Baltimore, Md., Penguin Books, 1950), p. 123.
18 Major John Cartwright, *Take Your Choice!* (London, 1776) and *American Independence: The Interest and Glory of Great Britain* (London, 1774; expanded edn, 1775).
19 Richard Price, *Observations on the Nature of Civil Liberty, the principles of Government, and the justice and policy of the war with America* (London, 1776). At least sixteen editions of this work appeared in 1776, including eleven in London.
20 G. M. Trevelyan, *British History in the Nineteenth Century and After: 1782–1919* (New York, Harper Torchbooks, 1966), p. 18.
21 *Works*, x, pp. 63–6; Bentham to Richard Clark (16 August 1768), *Correspondence*, ii, p. 130; Bentham to John Lind (2 September 1776), *Correspondence*, ii, pp. 341–4.
22 *Works*, ii, p. 271 (*Leading Principles of the Constitutional Code*).
23 Bentham to the Earl of Shelburne (18 July 1781), *The Correspondence of Jeremy Bentham, January 1781 to October 1788*, ed. Ian R. Christie (London, The Athlone Press, 1971), pp. 26–7. Further references to this work will be cited as *Correspondence*, iii.
24 *Works*, i, p. 295 (*A Fragment on Government*); *IPML*, pp. 307–11 and Bentham's remark of 1823 quoted at p. 281 fn.; *OLG*, p. 81.
25 UC 69, pp. 161, 215.
26 UC 69, pp. 112–13, 118, 120–3, 155–9.
27 *OLG*, p. 238 fn. d.

28 ibid., p. 5; *Works*, I, pp. 272–83 (*A Fragment on Government*).
29 UC 69, p. 177.
30 UC 63, p. 78.
31 UC 69, p. 166; see also p. 31.
32 UC 100, p. 12.
33 UC 69, pp. 176–7, 180, 200; *Works*, I, pp. 280–1, 289 (*A Fragment on Government*).
34 UC 141, pp. 138–9. See Sir Lewis Namier, *The Structure of Politics at the Accession of George III*, 2nd edn (London, Macmillan, 1960), pp. 128–9.
35 Bentham to the Earl of Shelburne (18 July 1781), *Correspondence*, III, pp. 28–9; UC 169, p. 1 (item 22).
36 UC 27, pp. 97, 105; UC 69, p. 188.
37 UC 63, p. 8. Also UC 27, pp. 45, 97, 105, 154; UC 32, pp. 158–61; UC 69, p. 127; UC 87, pp. 109, 124–6.
38 UC 69, p. 28. Also UC 27, pp. 16, 144; UC 69, pp. 59, 148, 170; UC 169, p. 76; *IPML*, p. 70.
39 *Works*, I, p. 289 (*A Fragment on Government*); *Comment on the Commentaries*, pp. 211–12; UC 70, p. 176; UC 97, p. 6; UC 107, pp. 6–9; UC 141, p. 43.
40 Bentham to Richard Clark (16 August 1768), *Correspondence*, I, p. 130; Bentham to Samuel Bentham (5 June 1780), *Correspondence*, II, pp. 457–8.
41 *OLG*, pp. 8–9.
42 Charles D. Tarlton, 'The Overlooked Strategy of Bentham's *Fragment on Government*', *Political Studies*, vol. XX (December 1972), p. 397. Cf. L. Burkholder, 'Tarlton on Bentham's *Fragment on Government*', *Political Studies*, vol. XXI (December 1973), pp. 523–6.
43 UC 27, p. 63.
44 W. Stark, Introduction, *Jeremy Bentham's Economic Writings*, ed. W. Stark, 3 vols (London, George Allen & Unwin, 1952–4), vol. III, p. 54.
45 ibid., vol. III, pp. 57–8. Bentham's remark is quoted by Stark, Introduction, *Economic Writings*, I, p. 20. See also pp. 117–18.
46 UC 87, pp. 70–1, 118; UC 169, p. 2.
47 UC 27, p. 141.
48 *Works*, IV, p. 375 (*Draught for the Organization of Judicial Establishments*); UC 87, p. 71; *OLG*, p. 70 fn. p.
49 Bentham to Samuel Bentham (18 May 1775), *Correspondence*, I, p. 235.
50 Bentham to Samuel Bentham (13–17 January 1777), *Correspondence*, II, p. 3.
51 UC 27, pp. 1, 4, 26, 55, 102; UC 69, p. 187; UC 87, p. 122; UC 169, pp. 98–9.
52 UC 169, p. 74.
53 See John Norris, *Shelburne and Reform* (London, Macmillan, 1963), pp. 141–3, as well as Bentham's letters to Shelburne throughout *Correspondence*, II–III.
54 Cf. *OLG*, pp. 232–41; *Works*, I, p. 289 (*A Fragment on Government*); *IPML*, p. 119; *Comment on the Commentaries*, p. 214; and the references cited in n. 51 of this chapter.
55 From George Wilson to Bentham (26 February 1787), *Correspondence*, III, p. 526.
56 UC 27, pp. 105–6, 123–4.
57 T. L. Sprigge, Introduction, *Correspondence*, I, p. xxxiv.
58 J. H. Burns, 'Bentham and the French Revolution', *The Transactions of The Royal Historical Society*, 5th series, vol. 16 (1966, pp. 95–114), p. 95. I am greatly indebted to Professor Burns' article for the discussion which follows.

59 ibid., p. 97.
60 ibid., pp. 97–8.
61 Quoted in and translated from the French by Mary Mack, *Jeremy Bentham: An Odyssey of Ideas 1748–1792* (London, Heinemann, 1962), p. 449. The 'essay on Representation' is in UC 170, pp. 87–121. Related material from this period may be found throughout UC 170 as well as in UC 126, pp. 1–18 and UC 127, pp. 1–19.
62 Halévy, *The Growth of Philosophic Radicalism*, trans. Mary Morris (Boston, Mass., The Beacon Press, 1955), pp. 166–9.
63 Mack, op. cit., pp. 440–1.
64 Burns, 'Bentham and the French Revolution', op. cit., p. 110.
65 ibid., p. 107.

Chapter III

Polity and Economy

Not the least cause of Bentham's reaction to the French Revolution was that the French National Assembly came to lay 'violent hands on private property'.[1] Bentham believed that the selfish and dissocial passions are the great enemies of public peace. Necessary as the selfish passions are to the survival of each individual, and thereby to the survival of the human species, they nevertheless ought to be feared. They are more apt to be in excess than in defect. They need to be restrained rather than developed. The Jacobins, in speaking of equal rights to property, were inflaming those selfish and dissocial passions, and encouraging each man to see in every other man his 'enemy' and his 'prey';[2] and they were doing so in pursuit of an impossible goal. The notion of any permanent equality in respect to property was nonsensical, for the moment equality was established it would collapse immediately. Some men simply are more adroit and more ambitious than others. Only perpetual meddling in respect to property could, in theory, maintain equality. But such meddling would be despotic and ruinous. It would be despotic because, flagrantly and without reason, it would neglect the important principle that each man is the best judge of his own interest. It would be ruinous because it would destroy any chance for development in the economic sphere. In the atmosphere created by such meddling, there would be no motive on the part of individuals to undertake any enterprise which might lead to increased wealth since such wealth would only be seized and redistributed immediately upon its creation. The result would be economic ruin, which would be detrimental to the poor and not only the rich. In neither sense, then, could such a project be conducive to the greatest happiness of the greatest number.[3]

Bentham's rejection of the 'socialist' or 'anarchic' implications of the French Revolution was only a reassertion of the *laissez faire* position he had taken in what is still his best known economic writing, the *Defence of Usury*, published in 1787. The *Defence of Usury* was written as a result of rumours, which Bentham heard while living in Russia, that Pitt was considering reducing the legal rate of interest from 5 to 4 per cent. Bentham immediately set about drafting a series of letters which argued not merely against the inutility of such a reduction but on 'behalf of the *liberty of making one's own terms in money-bargains*',[4] entirely free from any governmental restrictions whatsoever on the interest rate. In taking such a stand, Bentham knew that he was going beyond Adam Smith in arguing the case for *laissez faire*. Smith had held that the rate of interest ought not to be determined by the workings of the market place alone. To allow this would throw 'the greater part of the money which was to be lent' into the hands of 'prodigals and projectors, who alone would be willing to give this high interest'. The consequence would be to keep money from those 'sober people' who would be 'most likely to make a profitable and advantageous use of it, and [throw it] into those [hands] which were most likely to waste and destroy it'.[5]

While willing to admit that the prevention of prodigality 'is a proper object' for legislation, Bentham did not think that restrictions on the rate of interest were particularly conducive to that end. Moreover, the prevention of prodigality by any measure, however defensible, was not an essential undertaking:

> To prevent our doing mischief to one another, it is but too necessary to put bridles into all our mouths: it is necessary to the tranquillity and very being of society: but that the tacking of leading-strings upon the backs of grown persons, in order to prevent their doing themselves a mischief, is not necessary either to the being or tranquillity of society, however conducive to its well-being, I think cannot be disputed. Such paternal, or, if you please, maternal, care, may be a good work, but it certainly is but a work of supererogation.[6]

Although not simply adverse to paternalism in the case of the prodigal, Bentham was strongly opposed to it in respect to projectors. He thought that Smith had been misled, and was misleading others, by 'the tyranny of sounds' in his condemnation of projectors. To ask whether it was 'fit to restrain projects and projectors', given the current meaning of the terms, was 'as much as to ask, whether it be fit to restrain rashness, and folly, and absurdity, and knavery, and waste'.[7] Such rhetoric was both absurd and unfair: 'for think, Sir, let me beg of you, whether whatever is now the *routine* of trade was not, at its commencement, *project*? whether whatever is now *establishment*, was not, at one time, innovation?'[8] Projectors, in fact, have been the great benefactors of the nation. Through their courageous innovations, they have been the founders of 'that host of manufactures, which we both exult in as the causes and ingredients of national prosperity'.[9] Unfortunately, under the existing law, the continued growth and progress of the economy depended on those willing to violate the legal restrictions on interest rates: on projectors willing to borrow, and usurers willing to lend at higher interest rates than the law allowed. Such higher rates were necessary to permit high risk ventures to proceed, ventures which would contribute, in many instances, to the future prosperity of the nation. Thus the benefactors of the nation, projectors and usurers alike, were held in low esteem and threatened with punishment upon the unproven and the unprovable assumption that the legislator could know better than the individuals concerned what might be in their own best interest. Bentham's argument against restrictive interest rates, then, was based on the notion that 'no simplicity, short of absolute idiotism, can cause the individual to make a more groundless judgment, then the legislator . . . would have made for him'.[10] The individual, either lender or borrower, has at his disposal more concrete information than the legislator can conceivably have, and he has more of an active interest in seeing to it that the bargain he strikes is advantageous. The legislator cannot know the particular circumstances which cause a person, whether because of indigence or innovativeness, to be willing to borrow money at more than the current market rate. It was only prejudice rooted in the Christian notion of the virtue of self-denial for its own sake (to say nothing of Christian hostility toward Jews), reinforced by the misconceptions of Aristotle about the barren nature of money, which had misled even Smith, causing him to condemn projectors and usurers and to condone government interference in the free market where that interference could do no good though it would cause considerable harm.[11]

Bentham's stand in the *Defence of Usury* and his ardent defence of property against the excesses of the French Revolution led for a long time to the view that he was a dogmatic adherent to the *laissez faire* school of economics. This view was considerably reinforced by the fact that both James Mill and David Ricardo, much better known for their work in economics than Bentham, considered themselves to be his supporters. Thus both in his intellectual predecessor, Smith, and in his descendants, Bentham seems to have been fully within that lineage known as classical economic theory. Elie Halévy thought that Bentham's adherence to the *laissez faire* school involved him in a fundamental contradiction with the position he had taken in legal theory. According to Halévy, Bentham's belief in the predominance of egoistic motives compelled him to explain how any society managed to persist and not degenerate, immediately upon formation, into the Hobbesian war of all against all. For Halévy, there were two alternative possibilities. On the one hand, there is 'the thesis of the natural identity of interests' which maintains that while 'the predominating motives in human nature are egoistic' the very fact that 'the human species lives and survives' indicates 'that the various egoisms harmonise of their own accord and automatically bring about the good of the species'.[12] There is little need, then, for any superior power or authority to intervene to compel men to co-operate. This notion allegedly receives its prototypical formulation in Smith's famous remark about the 'invisible hand':

> As every individual, therefore, endeavours as much as he can both to employ his capital in the support of domestic industry, and so to direct that industry that its produce may be of the greatest value; every individual necessarily labours to render the annual revenue of the society as great as he can. He generally, indeed, neither intends to promote the public interest, not knows how much he is promoting it. By preferring the support of domestic to that of foreign industry, he intends only his own security; and by directing that industry in such a manner as its produce may be of the greatest value, he intends only his own gain, and he is in this, as in many other cases, led by an invisible hand to promote an end which was no part of his intention.[13]

Thus, in Bentham's terminology, each man in pursuing his own egoistic interest, 'his own security' and 'his own gain', automatically brings about the greatest happiness of the greatest number. According to Halévy, Bentham adhered to the theory of the natural identification of interests in economic theory; in respect to legal theory he adhered to 'the principle of the artificial identification of interests' which holds 'that it is the business of the legislator to bring about this identification' of interests through the use of law and, ultimately, force. Thus, in areas other than economics, Bentham generally appealed to 'the legislator to solve, by means of a well-regulated application of punishments, the great problems of morals' by identifying 'the interest of the individual with the interest of the community'.[14]

The idea that *laissez faire* 'was a vital article of the utilitarian creed', as A. V. Dicey argued in his significantly entitled lecture, 'The Period of Benthamism or Individualism',[15] went largely unchallenged for a long period of time. More recent scholarship, however, has pointed to the fact that Bentham's followers played an important role in such reforms as the Factory Act and the Poor Law which set England on the road toward a centralised welfare state. Indeed, J. Bartlet Brebner has argued that 'the extensive state intervention of that time' was 'basically Benthamite – Benthamite in the sense of conforming closely to that forbidding, detailed blueprint for a collectivist state, the *Constitutional Code*, which was written between 1820 and 1832'.[16] Brebner's argument has received some support from the improved texts of Bentham's economic writings which the Bowring edition, as is so often the case, badly mangled; as well as from the discovery of works which Bowring did not publish in the *Works* at all. But Brebner's notion that Bentham turned to collectivism after 1809 when he became angered over the Government's failure to adopt his Panopticon prison reform is as misleading as the view it seeks to replace.

From his early years, Bentham had expressed approval for at least limited government intervention in the sphere of economics. In 1773, for example, his brother had written to him concerning an invention made by a friend. Sam wondered whether the invention should be put into practice, particularly since it seemed likely that it would make certain labourers redundant. Bentham responded that there was no doubt in his mind that the project was worthy of pursuit, but he added, in a remark worthy of note for those who still believe he thought precise hedonic calculations were easy, that 'I need not tell you that it is impossible to form any tolerable aestimate of the quantity of happiness that the saving, supposing the exact sum of it could be known, would produce in this way. We are not however to conclude that this quantity, because difficult to adjust, is unreal or inconsiderable.'[17] Addressing himself to the possibility that the invention might cause unemployment, he argued that since the state 'ought to regard every one of it's members . . . with an equal eye', then 'a condition *sine qua non*' of accepting the project ought to be 'to secure a subsistence to all such persons as being thrown entirely out of employment, would otherwise be deprived of it: for it can hardly be, that the accession of happiness, comfort, etc. (call it what you will) to those to whose benefit the saving accrues, can compensate the sum of the distress experienced by a number of workmen in such a situation'.[18] Thus the state had a positive responsibility toward the unemployed, a notion also expressed in Bentham's 'Commonplace Book' in 1776. Reflecting on the problem of temporary stagnation of trade or manufacturing 'which leaves vast numbers at a time without employment, and without subsistence', he proposed a remedy in 'public works to be set on foot in the neighbourhood of manufacturing towns: to be carried on by none but manufacturers out of employment'.[19] Such works might include the digging of canals, the deepening of harbours and the making of roads, and W. Stark is surely correct in describing the proposal as 'humanitarian', 'practical' and 'progressive not to say revolutionary' in nature.[20]

In fact, Bentham consistently disowned any revolutionary attacks on private property throughout his lifetime, and for this reason it is as misleading to call him a collectivist as it is to see him as a strict adherent to the *laissez faire* school. If a collectivist is 'one who adheres to the theory that land and the means of production should be owned by the community for the benefit of the people as a whole',[21] then Bentham was never a collectivist. He believed that government should interfere with private ownership only on exceptional occasions and he never thought there were grounds, save in very rare cases, for actual government ownership. He opposed, as unnecessary, existing and proposed governmental attempts to encourage productivity through bounties or protectionist measures, and he condemned price controls as absurd. Generally speaking, his model was the market place, freed from governmental restraints. But this did not lead him to dogmatic and rigid opposition to defensible governmental policies designed to promote the greatest happiness of the greatest number. The basic position taken in the *Defence of Usury* was precisely the same position which he had taken in respect to penal legislation: the burden of proof is always on those who would meddle with freedom of choice.[22] Those who favoured restricting the interest rate had given no proof to show that to do so promoted the greatest happiness of the greatest number. They acted either out of prejudice or on the basis of reasons which were spurious or inadequate. But the fact that the defenders of a legally fixed interest rate had failed to give adequate reasons in no way precluded that, in other cases, sufficient reasons might exist for government intervention. The rule, then, was the free market but exceptions to that rule might exist, though those exceptions must be justified with solid reasons grounded on the principle of utility. Thus Bentham was willing to consider, at least in theory, that the government might be right in placing high taxes on luxury items such as jewellery. Jewels are purchased not so much for the pleasure they give in themselves but for the pleasure to be gained from ostentation. Such ostentation causes emulation by others. 'A custom of this sort when it has once got footing lays people under a kind of obligation of conforming to it, not for any satisfaction it affords them, but to avoid contempt. If they were relieved from this obligation they might spend their money more to their satisfaction in another way', and in doing so they might give a boost to domestic trade.[23] Moreover, since the rule even in the *Defence of Usury* was qualified by the condition that the bargain was struck by persons who had their eyes open, Bentham could argue elsewhere that laws to prevent fraud by establishing uniform standards of weights, measures, and purity in foods were defensible.[24]

Bentham knew that the principle that the greatest happiness of the greatest number is the proper end of government was too general to be of much use in concrete cases. Accordingly he proposed that specific determinations should be made in the light of what he called the four subsidiary ends of legislation: security, subsistence, abundance and equality.

> This division has not all the exactness which might be desired. The limits which separate these objects are not always easy to be determined.

> They approach each other at different points, and mingle together. But it is enough to justify this division, that it is the most complete we can make; and that, in fact, we are generally called to consider each of the objects which it contains, separately and distinct from all the others.[25]

Because, particularly in practice, these subsidiary ends do interact with one another, the legislator must have some way of deciding which end should be given preference. Bentham argued that the two most important subsidiary ends are security and subsistence, while abundance and equality 'are manifestly of inferior importance'.[26] Without security there would be neither abundance nor an approximation to meaningful equality. Without some assurance that property will be protected, people would make little or no effort to create new wealth. The 'principal object of law' is, therefore, to take care of security for, in doing so, the other ends will be served as well:

> Without law there is no security; and, consequently, no abundance, and not even a certainty of subsistence; and the only equality which can exist in such a state of things is an equality of misery.
>
> To form a just idea of the benefits of law, it is only necessary to consider the condition of savages. They strive incessantly against famine, which sometimes cuts off entire tribes. Rivalry for subsistence produces among them the most cruel wars; and, like beasts of prey, men pursue men, as a means of sustenance. The fear of this terrible calamity silences the softer sentiments of nature; pity unites with insensibility in putting to death the old men who can hunt no longer.[27]

This was a characteristic argument of the age, one which had its roots in Hobbes and Locke. Without the protection given to property by law, life would be 'solitary, poor, nasty, brutish, and short'.[28] By providing security for life and property, government establishes an environment in which man may not only survive but civilisation and the softer sentiments of nature may develop. Thus the principal task of government is to see that individuals do not threaten each other's life or invade each other's property; and government itself must not take any unwarranted action which would threaten life or property.

Bentham often carried his argument about the pre-eminence of security quite far. Although opposed to that 'civil inequality' known as slavery, he argued against its immediate abolition because to do so might threaten the security of property, and he added that men 'who are rendered free by . . . gradations, will be much more capable of being so than if you had taught them to tread justice under foot, for the sake of introducing a new social order'.[29] At the same time, he did not believe that there was any natural and inviolable right to property. All rights are created by law and they are only properly created when they are conducive to the greatest happiness of the greatest number. Established rights, even if unjust, may have to be respected and only gradually altered. But there is no absolute right to property. At the minimum, the very necessity of providing for security requires government to interfere with property. To provide for a police force to protect against domestic threats to property and a military to protect against external threats requires money, and money typically is raised by taxation. Bentham distinguished between a sharp and sudden attack on property, and a fixed, regular and necessary deduction from the wealth of the people which was required to support the operations of the government.[30]

Nor did he restrict such deductions to the function of providing security. In normal times the legislature need do nothing to provide for subsistence. As long as it protects each individual while he labours and secures for him the fruits of that labour, each individual will take care of his own subsistence and that of his family. But times are not always normal. Even 'the most diligent and the most virtuous' may at times be thrown into a condition of indigence and be unable to take care of their own subsistence.[31] Parents may die, leaving children who are too young to work. The elderly may find their meagre savings inadequate to maintain existence. Bad weather may put food in critically short supply. The collapse of an industry may throw labourers out of work for more or less prolonged periods of time. If, when such situations occur, savings and voluntary contributions were sufficient to support subsistence, then it would be unwise for the government to act. But even a brief examination shows that neither savings nor charity are sufficient. Even the greatest effort barely provides daily support for the poor, so how can they be expected to save? Nor can one count on voluntary contributions which must always be uncertain and which place an inequitable burden on the more humane members of the populace:

> This supply for the wants of the poor is levied entirely at the expense of the more humane and the more virtuous, often without any proportion to their means; while the avaricious calumniate the poor, to cover their refusal with a varnish of system and of reason. Such an arrangement is a favour granted to selfishness, and a punishment to humanity, that first of virtues.[32]

Moreover, it is not always the deserving poor who receive the benefits of charity but rather the importuner, the flatterer, the liar who mixes boldness with baseness to succeed while 'the virtuous poor, devoid of artifice, and preserving their honour in their poverty' go hungry.[33]

Thus it is necessary for government, on a variety of occasions, to provide for subsistence. The only question in Bentham's mind was how this could be done in the most appropriate manner. How might one provide for relief without threatening the security of property of those who, in some way, must be made to carry the burden? How to provide relief so as not to reward idleness and punish industry? 'In respect of the comfortableness of the provision it is very difficult to hit the proper medium. To fall short of the mark is inhuman: go beyond it and you give a bounty upon idleness in prejudice of industry.'[34] Bentham, ever the projector, devised a number of schemes which he felt would be useful in coping with those dire situations where the very lives of some part of the citizenry were threatened by the want of subsistence.

As has been shown above, Bentham had suggested as early as the 1770s that the government might maintain employment, and thereby provide subsistence, through public work projects. By the 1790s, his thinking had turned in somewhat different directions. In a series of essays, some published and some not, he proposed a system of agricultural communes for the south of England, and a system of Industry Houses, both designed for those who were, for whatever reason, unable to maintain subsistence by themselves.[35] It is impossible to give an adequate summary of the incredible details Bentham incorporated into these plans although, as is so often the case with his proposals, the details are fascinating, at times because they are shrewdly devised, at other times because they are so abhorrent to contemporary modes of thought, at yet other times for both reasons. The most important point is that both projects were to provide care for the indigent, as distinct from the working poor, by providing work for them under strict supervision and, if necessary, compulsion. Both projects were designed to encourage the beneficiaries to return to the normal labour market as soon as possible. Care must be taken to insure that the lot of those who benefited from the programmes was not superior to the lot of the poor who remained at work in the open market. To fail to do so would be to reward those able but unwilling to work, and this would be to the detriment of the industrious poor whose own situation, in the nature of things, was always but one step removed from actual indigence. Thus the worker in the free market ought to receive higher wages than those working in the Industry Houses, and he ought to have the freedom to spend his wages in ways not permitted to the latter. 'The demand created by *indigence* can never be said to extend beyond the absolute *necessaries* of life. For, generally speaking, the ability of those who are maintained by their *own* labour, does little more than pass this limit: & beyond it there are *no bounds*.'[36] Accordingly, governments are well advised to restrict the provisions supplied to the indigent and warranted in setting down conditions of compliance in return for relief. Such conditions might include the prohibition of alcoholic beverages and the requirement of a uniform dress, as well as any other rules which 'in its *own* judgment, are conducive, to the benefit, either of the individual *himself*, or of the *community* at large, at whose expense he is to be relieved'.[37]

Such rules and regulations might seem to fly in the face of the dictum that each man is the best judge of his own interest. But, as Bentham's argument makes clear, it is the greatest happiness of the greatest number which is being sought, and that may well require that a minority give up certain of its freedoms in return for appropriate benefits. Surely an individual faced with the alternative of starvation might well find it in his best interest to submit to such regulations, particularly when at the first opportunity he could return to the free market. But Bentham also seems to have presumed at times that the fact that certain individuals regularly become indigent suggests *prima facie* evidence that they are imprudent. Still they are exceptions to the general rule of prudence. Certainly Bentham did not argue that every individual who was indigent was imprudent. He recognised that there were situations which overwhelmed even the most prudent. In respect to them, the regulations of the houses were justified by the need to see that the imprudence of the truly imprudent did not infect the unfortunate prudent individuals, and lead them to believe that imprudence was being rewarded in any way.[38] Moreover, it should be recognised that Bentham's willingness to provide subsistence for those who were most flagrant in their imprudence clearly distinguished him from those who felt that such imprudence should not be relieved even if it meant starvation. Bentham argued that such a policy was incompatible with simple humanity and, indeed, with the very security of property itself. Only vengeance would dictate such harshness as allowing others to starve when it could be prevented. Nor would such vengefulness in any way correct the imprudence, either in the present or in the future, for few are likely to believe that their imprudence will lead to their starvation. From the standpoint of humanity, confirmed by utility, one ought not to stand by and let one's fellow man suffer if one can in any way assist him, whether he is worthy of assistance or not. Moreover, not the least utility in doing so is that to fail to give assistance might provoke such individuals to attack private property, an attack which, particularly if it were to spread, could only be put down by brutal and brutalising means.[39]

Characteristically, Bentham thought that his plans for the relief of the indigent might be so devised to serve a lengthy series of corollary ends.

The Industry Houses might serve to take care of orphans, foundlings and abandoned children. Education might be provided within the Houses. They could become medical dispensaries not only for the inhabitants but for the independent poor in the vicinity. A medical curator could offer instruction in midwifery. A Poor Man's Bank might be established to encourage both the inhabitants of the Houses and the independent poor to save; to provide them with an inexpensive means of transferring funds from one part of the country to another in order, for example, to assist needy relatives. Provisions might be made to secure to the independent poor low-interest loans to aid them in times of temporary distress. Loans might be advanced to those who had nothing to pledge but their good character; they might even be granted to the independent poor to allow them to take out a mortgage on a home of their own.[40] Rather obviously, these proposals incorporate a great number of very advanced ideas for providing assistance not only to the indigent but to the great majority who were the working poor. They indicate rather clearly why it is exceedingly misleading to see Bentham as a mere adherent to *laissez faire* economics. In fact, despite his general opposition to price regulations, Bentham could and did argue that, in order to maintain subsistence, the government might be justified in establishing a maximum price for grain as well as regulations prohibiting the export of food during times of scarcity, though he thought it would be more desirable for the government to magazine grain during good harvest years.[41]

If Bentham was convinced that government intervention was justified in order to maintain subsistence, he was much less sure whether such intervention was either necessary or desirable in respect to the subsidiary ends of abundance and equality. He believed that, with rare exceptions, the government could do little to promote abundance. Protecting the means of subsistence apart, a free market ought to be established both internally and externally. Import and export regulations should be abolished, as well as government support for industry either in the form of protected monopolies or government subsidies. Abundance will most likely occur if the government does nothing except provide protection for private property and industry. The individual investor is most likely to be the best judge as to what industry or occupation is most likely to increase his own wealth, and therewith the wealth of the nation. Government support, in contrast, is all too likely to flow to antiquated and obsolete areas of industry – a classic case of throwing good money after bad. To be certain, government might be able to gather information which would assist individual investors; patent protections should be given to encourage new inventions; and it might even be defensible to provide temporary protection for a nascent industry.[42] But the rule, with but few exceptions, was the free and unencumbered market place. Yet even here Bentham was undogmatic. Beginning in 1795–6, he investigated in detail the possibility that the establishment of government annuity notes might increase the circulation of money and help to pay off the national debt. In both cases, the possibility existed that capital would be freed for investment purposes. In a series of works he examined both the details which would be necessary to establish such notes, and the ramifications of such a policy not only in respect to capital flow but also in regard to the impact it would have on the currencies issued by the county banks and the Bank of England. He argued on behalf of the superior benefits of a nationally controlled currency, and, as has been noted by Stark, he went a long way along the road towards modern monetary policy. However, he ultimately dropped his plans, in part because of the want of a favourable response from the government of the day, in part because of a growing concern that the policy would have inflationary tendencies which would work particular hardship on people with fixed incomes, especially the elderly.[43]

The most unusual aspect of Bentham's considerations of the subsidiary ends is that he included equality at all. As has already been shown, he greatly feared any government-sponsored levelling tendency in respect to property and, accordingly, at one point at least he was willing to discount equality as a subsidiary goal in respect to economic policy.[44] Still, even at the height of his reaction to the French Revolution, he recognised that 'the condition of a body is the situation of the greater part of the individuals who compose it', and that, therefore, 'the general rule, in as far as particular dispositions are thought fit to be subjected to a general rule, the general rule, were it necessary there should be one, ought to wear a democratical tinge'.[45] In general, however, he did not believe it was necessary for government to do much in the way of promoting equality since he believed, following Smith, that the working of a free market would, in and of itself, go a long way toward establishing relative equality over a period of time. Those who have wealth tend, human nature being what it is, to become inactive and indolent. Although they may desire still greater wealth, there is no substantial incentive to cause them to work hard to acquire it, while there are substantial motives to lead them to enjoy the wealth they already have. On the other hand, those who are relatively poor are anxious to better their lot. They are the active elements within society, and, in the course of time, they (taken as a group) will gain wealth while the rich will lose it.[46]

This may have been a naïve view both of human nature and of the workings of the free market. But once again Bentham was not quite willing to leave everything to chance. He recognised that inherited wealth might disrupt the normal workings of the market. The central difficulty confronting any government attempt to redistribute wealth was that it would constitute a dangerous shock to existing expectations. Taking any portion of wealth, no matter how insignificant, might create a sense of general insecurity in respect to property and the fear that further and more radical encroachments might be made. This fear might result in economic stagnation or the flight of capital from the country.[47] But what if a plan could be devised which would give no shock to established expectations? Bentham believed that he had found such a plan in his proposal to tax estates. Inheritances left to immediate relatives would go untaxed and there would be certain other exceptions as well.[48] But any inheritance not covered by the exceptions would be taxed at the rate of 50 per cent. Since everyone would know in advance that this was the law, no expectations would develop which might be shocked. The money received from such a tax would not go directly to the poor but would be used to replace highly inequitable taxes such as those on law proceedings, medical drugs, windows, soap and salt, all of which worked an undue hardship on the poor.[49]

Despite this and other brief efforts to work out a more equitable tax structure to finance government,[50] in general Bentham did not view the tax system as a means of redistributing the wealth of society. But it is interesting to note that there were elements in his general view of man which might have lent themselves to such a conclusion. It is no great step from arguing that an established and expected tax in respect to inheritance need give no shock to security, to wondering, given the subsidiary end of equality, whether or not a graduated income tax might be defensible on the same grounds. To be sure, such a tax, while being progressive, would have to be free from the dangers of being perceived, whether rightly or wrongly, as exorbitantly unfair to the wealthy or as being confiscatory in nature. Otherwise one would risk both giving undue pain to the rich and promoting a ruinous economic situation. But, as subsequent experience shows, it is not inconceivable that a defensible and acceptable (and for Bentham these two things were not the same) progressive income tax might be devised and used to support the kinds of programmes he advocated in respect to Industry Houses and agricultural communes. But in making such an argument, one runs up against two apparently conflicting axioms which Bentham held. In the first place:

> Sum for sum, and man for man, the suffering of him who incurrs a loss is always greater than the enjoyment of him who makes a gain: and the difference between this suffering and this enjoyment gives

> in this point of view the mischief of the measure. According to common estimation the gain, instead of being regarded as inferior to the loss, has hitherto been regarded as if it were clear: because in political arithmetic, blinded by passions or prejudices, men count but on one side. Reckoning the man whose fortune lies in the air or in some thing else besides money as every body, and his feelings as the only feelings worth attending to, and him whose fortune consists in ready money as nobody or as [a being] without feeling, or as one whose feelings are not worth regarding, what is gained by the one is carried to the side of national profit, while what is lost to the other is sunk in the account of national loss: and it is thus that bills given on to the nation by ministers for pretended services done to the nation are made out.[51]

On the basis of this argument, to take £10 from Smith to give it to Jones would cause Smith greater pain than the pleasure which would be given to Jones, and the result would be a diminution of overall happiness. But, on the other hand, Bentham also held to the principle of marginal or diminishing utility: though '*of two individuals with unequal fortunes, he who has the most wealth has the most happiness*' yet '*the excess in happiness of the richer will not be so great as the excess of his wealth*'.[52]

> Put on one side a thousand farmers, having enough to live upon, and a little more. Put on the other side a king, or, not to be encumbered with the cares of government, a prince, well portioned, himself as rich as all the farmers taken together. It is probable, I say, that his happiness is greater than the average happiness of the thousand farmers; but it is by no means probable that it is equal to the sum total of their happiness, or, what amounts to the same thing, a thousands times greater than the average happiness of one of them. It would be remarkable if his happiness were ten times, or even five times greater.[53]

On the basis of this principle it might be possible to argue that a tax on one so rich as a prince might cause him less pain than the pleasure which would be given to the poor, to say nothing of the farmers, by allocating to them a share of his wealth. At the minimum reconciling these two arguments would involve a very complicated calculation. But it is important to note that Bentham's thought did not move in that direction, and that, indeed, he opposed the notion of an income tax albeit on grounds largely unconnected with equality.[54] Bentham was still some years away from embracing political democracy and espousing a form of government which might consider making such calculations.

By 1804 he was turning away from economic subjects, and was to spend the next five years largely engrossed in his work on judicial evidence and prison reform, until in 1809, on his own recollection, he first came to argue for the necessity of democratic reform within the English Constitution.

Notes Chapter III

1 Samuel Bentham to Lord St Helens (8 July 1791), *Works*, x, p. 262.
2 *Works*, II, p. 497 (*Anarchical Fallacies*).
3 ibid., pp. 496–7, 503, 525–6, 529; *Works*, I, pp. 358–64 (*Of the Levelling System*).
4 *Economic Writings*, I, p. 129 (*Defence of Usury*).
5 Adam Smith, *The Wealth of Nations* (New York, The Modern Library, 1937), bk II, ch. IV, pp. 339–40.
6 *Economic Writings*, I, pp. 133–4 (*Defence of Usury*).
7 ibid., p. 169.
8 ibid., p. 172.
9 ibid., p. 179.
10 ibid., p. 140.
11 ibid., pp. 156–9.
12 Halévy, *The Growth of Philosophic Radicalism*, trans. Mary Morris (Boston, Mass., The Beacon Press, 1955), p. 15.
13 Smith, op. cit., bk. IV, ch. II, p. 423. The careful reader will note that Smith, by adding 'in many other cases', was not advancing the theory of the invisible hand as a universal rule. See Shirley Letwin, *The Pursuit of Certainty* (Cambridge, The University Press, 1965), pp. 146–7 fn. 1.
14 Halévy, op. cit., pp. 17–18.
15 A. V. Dicey, *Lectures on the Relation between Law and Public Opinion during the Nineteenth Century*, 2nd edn (London, Macmillan, 1924), p. 198 and pp. 126–210.
16 J. Bartlet Brebner, 'Laissez Faire and State Intervention in Nineteenth-Century Britain', *The Journal of Economic History: Supplement*, vol. VIII (1948), p. 62 and pp. 59–73 in general. There has been some controversy over the exact role played by Bentham's followers in the development of the modern British welfare state. See David Roberts, *Victorian Origins of the British Welfare State* (New Haven, Yale University Press, 1960), *passim*, and Geoffrey Finlayson, *Decade of Reform: England in the Eighteen Thirties* (New York, W. W. Norton, 1970), especially pp. 64–72.
17 Bentham to Samuel Bentham (4 November 1773), *Correspondence*, I, p. 167 and pp. 164–70 in general.
18 ibid., pp. 166–7.
19 Quoted from *Works*, x, p. 85 in *Economic Writings*, I, p. 13. It should be noted, to avoid confusion, that 'manufacturers' meant at the time persons who worked with their hands.
20 W. Stark, Introduction, *Economic Writings*, p. 13.
21 *Oxford Universal Dictionary*.
22 *Economic Writings*, I, p. 129 (*Defence of Usury*). Also ibid., pp. 229–31 (*Manual of Political Economy*).

23 UC 72, p. 67.
24 UC 87, p. 37.
25 *Theory of Legislation*, p. 96.
26 ibid., p. 98.
27 ibid., p. 109.
28 Thomas Hobbes, *Leviathan* (Oxford, Basil Blackwell, 1947), pt. I, ch. 13, p. 82. On Hobbes and Locke see Leo Strauss, *Natural Rights and History* (Chicago, University of Chicago Press, 1953), pp. 165–251.
29 *Theory of Legislation*, pp. 122–3.
30 ibid., pp. 109–13, 115–26; *Economic Writings*, I, pp. 328–37 (*Supply without Burthen*).
31 *Theory of Legislation*, pp. 127–8.
32 ibid., p. 130. Also UC 87, pp. 79–80.
33 *Theory of Legislation*, p. 131.
34 UC 87, p. 80.
35 'Tracts on Poor Law and Pauper Management' was published in Arthur Young's *Annals of Agriculture* (1797) and reprinted with additions in *Works*, VIII, pp. 357–439, and the unpublished 'Essays relative to the subject of the Poor Law' and 'Essays on the Subject of the Poor Laws' in UC 152, pp. 1–218 and UC 153, pp. 1–77. There is additional material on the subject of the poor and indigent throughout these boxes as well as in UC 154.
36 UC 153, p. 24.
37 UC 153, p. 26.
38 UC 152, pp. 13, 19–20; UC 153, pp. 25–6.
39 UC 152, pp. 13–20; UC 153, pp. 25–6.
40 UC 153, pp. 32–4, 36–41, 46–52. See also the drafts at UC 153, pp. 78–141.
41 *Economic Writings*, III, pp. 247–302 (*Defence of a Maximum*). In fact, as Lord Robbins demonstrated some years ago, many of the adherents to the school of classical economics have been unfairly portrayed as dogmatic and heartless thinkers. See Lionel Robbins, *The Theory of Economic Policy in English Classical Political Economy* (London, Macmillan, 1961).
42 See, for example, *Economic Writings*, I, pp. 211, 213–14 (*Colonies and Navy*) and pp. 228–9, 231-2, 238–60 (*Manual of Political Economy*).
43 See the discussion by Stark, Introduction, *Economic Writings*, II, pp. 7–113 and Bentham's various attempts to analyse monetary policy which are collected in that volume.
44 *Economic Writings*, I, p. 226 (*Manual of Political Economy*).
45 ibid., pp. 329–30 (*Supply without Burthen*).
46 *Theory of Legislation*, pp. 111–23. Cf. Smith, op. cit., bk I, ch. I, pp. 11–12; ch. VII, pp. 78–84; bk II, ch. III, pp. 314–32.
47 *Theory of Legislation*, pp. 109–11, 115–26. Cf. Stark, Introduction, *Economic Writings*, I, p. 64.
48 *Economic Writings*, I, pp. 283–7 (*Supply without Burthen*).
49 ibid., pp. 298–300.
50 *Economic Writings*, I, pp. 371–412 (*Tax with Monopoly and Proposal for a Mode of Taxation*).
51 ibid., pp. 239–40 (*Manual of Political Economy*). See also ibid., pp. 364–5 (*Supply without Burthen*).
52 *Theory of Legislation*, p. 103.
53 ibid., pp. 104–5. See *Economic Writings*, I, pp. 113–17.
54 *Economic Writings*, I, p. 380 (*Proposal for a Mode of Taxation*).

Chapter IV

The Making of a Democrat

The principle of utility, applied to the realm of politics, measures the goodness or badness of a government or constitution by its success or failure in protecting and promoting the greatest happiness of the greatest number of the inhabitants of a given state. Clearly there is nothing inherently democratic in the principle itself. It could be and was adhered to with perfect consistency by conservatives and liberals, and even by benevolent despots like Catherine the Great of Russia. Each adherent to the principle could maintain, at least in theory, that one or another form of government in fact best protected or promoted the greatest happiness of the greatest number. Or they might hold that forms of government are irrelevant to happiness:

> For Forms of Government let fools contest;
> Whate'er is best administer'd is best:[1]

Something along this latter line would seem best to describe Bentham's position for the better part of his life. For although, as has been shown, there were potentially democratic elements in Bentham's formulation of the principle of utility, such as the psychological axiom that each one is the best judge of his own interest and the inclusion of equality as one of the four subsidiary ends, nevertheless by his own insistence he did not give any prolonged attention to constitutional questions nor become a democrat until 1809.

When he began to devote attention to the subject, he attacked the English form of government with a passion which, on more than one occasion, bordered on excess; and during the period after 1809 he not only became a democrat but an increasingly radical one. What happened to shake his early complacency? There is a widely held view, best expressed by Halévy, that he was motivated by an ulcered bitterness over the English Government's treatment of his Panopticon proposal for prison reform: 'The disappointment and the distress which he suffered made him a democrat: in hatred of the monarch and his ministers, he became a deliberate enemy of monarchic and of aristocratic institutions.'[2]

There is no gainsaying the anger Bentham felt over the failure of the government to support his plans for prison reform. His feelings may well be assessed in the light of the rather enlarged hopes he had for the Panopticon scheme, hopes which he expressed in the following often quoted remark: '*Morals reformed – health preserved – industry invigorated – instruction diffused – public burthens lightened – Economy seated, as it were, upon a rock – the gordian knot of the Poor-Laws not cut, but untied – all by a simple idea in Architecture!*'[3]

Bentham had been interested in prison reform, as a natural extension of his interest in penal law reform, since his early years. In 1778, he published *A View of the Hard Labour Bill* which recommended changes in penal institutions in order to assist in the reformation of the prisoners as well as to provide for greater security.[4] But his real involvement only came after 1786–7. His brother, whom he was visiting in White Russia, had invented 'a mode of architecture, to which I gave the name of Panopticon, from the two Greek words, – one of which signified everything, the other a place of sight'.[5] The Panopticon design was devised by Sam to serve for the supervision of a large workshop. An inspector, stationed in a central lodge, could observe any given workman without that workman knowing whether or not he, in fact, was being watched. The idea was that the capacity of one inspector would be greatly increased. Each workman, believing that he might be seen at any time, would be more inclined to stick to his work and the consequence would be a considerable improvement in productivity. Bentham immediately saw the potential of the design for supervision in a prison, and to it he added the idea of contract management by private entrepreneurs as being more economical than government management:

> Taking in hand this idea, I made application of it for the purpose of the case in which the persons subjected to inspection, were placed in that situation, not only for the purpose of being subjected to direction, but also for the purpose of being made to suffer in the way of punishment: in a word, as a place of labour and confinement for convicts.
>
> To the carrying this design into effect, two requisites were necessary: – The first an appropriate form of architecture as above, and an appropriate plan of management, so organized as to draw from that mode of architecture, as far as practicable, all the advantages it was capable of affording. In the course of my reflections on this latter subject, I came to my conclusion, that the customary plan pursued in works instituted by Government, and carried on, on account of Government, was, in an eminent degree, ill adapted to the purpose: though to this general rule, particular exceptions there might be; but to the particular purpose then in hand, they had no

> application. Accordingly, management by contract, I became convinced, was the only plan that afforded a probability of good success.[6]

He elaborated on the implications of the design and the principle of contract management in a series of 'letters' written in 1787 and published in 1791 as *Panopticon, or The Inspection House*, to which he added two lengthy postscripts which detailed the building even down to the size and shape of the doors and windows. The details of such projects always fascinated Bentham, much, it must be said, to his brother's occasional distress.[7] But on this occasion, at least, there was a more practical purpose in such elaboration since Bentham hoped that he might be the person to operate such a prison under contract from the government. He saw such a model prison as an ideal place for developing methods of what today would be called behavioural modification in reforming the prisoners, and in preventing crime by using the prisoners as examples of the consequences of ill behaviour. On this latter count, he particularly hoped to impress on young children, who would be brought to visit the prison, the price to be paid for criminal activity. He felt that the use of graphic symbols over the cells would develop powerful associations in the minds of the young and act as effective deterents to keep them from wrongdoing.[8]

Nor did Bentham feel that the usefulness of the Panopticon scheme would be limited to prisons. He believed, as he suggested in the original 'letters', that it might be adapted for Houses of Industry, work houses, poor houses, manufactories, madhouses, lazarrettos, hospitals, and schools.[9] But for the next two decades and more, he concentrated on its utility for a prison, working diligently to explain, defend and develop its advantages over the existing practices of penal colonies and hulks. In a manner quite unusual for him, he saw through to completion several works in addition to the original 'letters': *Letters to Lord Pelham*, published in 1802, and *A Plea for the Constitution*, printed in 1803 and published together with the former work in 1812 as *Panopticon versus New South Wales*.[10] Although the government encouraged him on more than one occasion, negotiations dragged on for years until they were finally squelched by the decision to establish a prison to be operated by the government itself.

Although Bentham was compensated financially for expenses he had incurred, there was no way of compensating the profound disappointment he experienced over the end to the great expectations he had raised in his own mind over the benefits he thought the plan would bring to prisoners, to society and to himself. In *A Plea for the Constitution*, he demonstrated the lengths he was willing to go in advocating his cause. He denounced the system of transporting prisoners to penal colonies in the name of '*natural justice*', and, while admitting that many of the actions of the governors in New South Wales were defensible in the name of '*abstract utility*', he nevertheless held them to be illegal and unconstitutional. He claimed that particular measures neglected the 'rights' of the prisoners and that resistance to such measures was 'a matter of *right*'.[11] Strange words coming from the author of *Anarchical Fallacies* which had so uncompromisingly condemned as pernicious appeals to natural right and natural justice. Given the strength of feelings expressed in *A Plea for the Constitution*, it is no wonder that Bentham turned against the government which had thwarted his plans. But he did not stop there. According to a common view, supported by Bentham's own testimony, he believed that the King personally had intervened to scuttle his plans. As Bowring tells the story:

> In the year 1789, an attempt was made by Great Britain, or by the King of Great Britain, to break up the alliance between Russia and Denmark. The pretext was the restoration of the balance of the power, and the retention by Russia of Oczakow, which had been taken from the Turks by the Russians. In the *Gazette de Leyde*, letters were written under a feigned name by George the Third himself, urging the King of Denmark the propriety of his breaking his engagements with Russia, and associating himself with the policy then pursued.[12]

When 'a private communication of Mr Elliott our minister, at Copenhagen, to the Danish court, obtained publicity', Bentham responded by sending letters signed 'Anti-Machiavel' to the *Public Advertiser*, 'sharply attacking the policy of his . . . royal opponent'.[13] As Bentham reportedly told Bowring in later years:

> Who Anti-Machiavel was, became soon known to this same 'best of kings', for that was the title which the prolific virtues of his wife had conferred upon him. Imagine how he hated me. Millions wasted were among the results of his vengeance. In a way too long to state, he broke the faith of the Admiralty Board pledged to my brother. After keeping me in hot water more years than the siege of Troy lasted, he broke the faith of Parliament to me. But for him all the paupers in the country, as well as all the prisoners in the country, would have been in my hands. A penal code drawn by me would have become law. Of the Panopticon establishment, the character to which it owed its chief value in my eye, was that of a means leading to that end.[14]

If the King thwarted Bentham's plans in vengeance, Bentham, in his turn, directed his vengeance not only against the King but against the whole monarchic establishment. His hostility toward the monarchy needed only a fillip to convert him into a democrat, and that was provided when he met James Mill sometime in 1808 or 1809.[15]

The idea that Bentham became a democrat solely out of his hostility toward the King, although widely believed, is almost certainly wrong. In the first place it does not square with the chronology of events. Bentham's bitterness over the government's dilatory procedure was expressed as early as 1802–3, long before he became a democrat, and the end to his hopes did not come until 1811, two years after he had embraced the belief in the necessity for democratic reform. Moreover, as the most severe of his recent critics has noted, it was Lord Lansdowne, formerly the Earl of Shelburne, who had told Bentham that it was the King who was his opponent and had signed a reply to the 'Anti-Machiavel' letters as 'Partizan'.

> At the time and for many years (indeed as late as 1809), Bentham refused to credit this identification, supposing it to be another ruse on Lansdowne's part to provoke him to a more Whiggish and anti-royalist position. . . . It was not until 1821, when he first committed to writing the theory of the royal plot, that he assumed as a matter of course that Lansdowne had been telling the truth.[16]

It is curious and ironic, nevertheless, that the belief persists that Bentham's conversion to democracy was a consequence of pernicious motives on his part. It is curious since it is so often believed by the same critics who condemn Bentham for holding that governors only act out of sinister interests and the worst of motives. It is ironic since Bentham himself condemned the attempt to judge the consequence of actions in the light of motives. Motives are difficult, perhaps impossible, to know and they are often, although not always, irrelevant to the beneficial or detrimental nature of the consequences of an action. As he noted, shortly after he became a democrat, it was likely there were some who embraced a plan of reform similar to his own, whose designs might well be suspect. But, as he added, a good measure ought not to be set aside simply because it is supported by bad men.[17] As Bentham knew:

> The field of motives is an open and ample field for the exercise not of mendacity only, but of bias. The tendency of bias is to attribute the greatest share, or rather the whole agency, in the production of the act, to a particular motive; to the exclusion of, or in preference to, whatever others may have concurred in the production of it. Few indeed that are able, scarce any that are willing, to give, on every

> occasion, a correct account of the state of the psychological force by which their conduct has been produced.[18]

The springs of human action are complex and they operate in 'proportions never the same for two days or two hours together'.[19] Bentham, despite a common myth to the contrary, was a complex man, and the reasons for his conversion to democracy are equally complex, his bitterness over the treatment of the Panopticon being only one of several causes.

Bentham himself saw the increasing patronage in the hands of the King as the central reason necessitating reformation of the Constitution. As was shown in Chapter II, he had been dismayed by the role which the Church of England played within the English Constitution, and now, once again, he returned to that theme. He repeated the charge that the use of oaths allowed the Church to corrupt both the intellect and the morals of the leading men of the community who passed under her tutelage. Whatever weakened the intellect and enervated morals contributed greatly toward increasing the power of the King. But the King's power was not increased only by the obsequiousness and insincerity which the Church planted in the hearts of men. It was also increased by the patronage which was placed in his hands in the form of various sinecures. The existence of those sinecures, as well as secular honours which the King could bestow, gave the monarch undue influence over the members of both Commons and Lords. This corruptive influence was worse than bribery, since people were too ready to believe that protections against its abuse resided in the House of Commons. In fact, a substantial minority in the House willingly went along with the King's plans simply out of indolence and obsequiousness, while enough others could be won over by the distribution of patronage to themselves or to their family and friends.[20] Thus party leaders were made dependent on the King, and through them he could control Parliament as a whole. One should not think that Bentham was arguing that patronage operated as an inducement to subservience simply in the form of money, for money was not the only incentive to office. To think that 'supposes that instead of there being as many sorts of motives as there are of pleasures and pains there is but one sort and that love of money: that power, reputation, dignity – faculty of serving friends – assurance of respect from strangers as well as friends – that these objects' of desire which are, in fact, 'so general have none of them any value'.[21]

Since Bentham had long been aware of the dangers posed by sinecures and the Church of England, why was it only now that those dangers led him to embrace the cause of parliamentary reform? Bentham was very much aware of what he called his previous 'self-conscious ignorance' in respect to reform, and admitted that had he been required to express an opinion it most likely would have gone against the necessity of reform. But what he now saw which he had not previously seen was that the influence of the King permitted him regularly to carry the majority in Parliament, irrespective of which party was in office.[22] This meant that, at the least, the King could prevent the passage of any legislation of which he did not approve and, at the most, that he could attain the adoption of legislation which he favoured, including legislation to increase his patronage power further and, therewith, his power in general. In fact, Bentham asserted, to render the King absolute nothing was wanting, nor had been wanting for more than twenty years, but skill and wisdom, little, if anything, beyong the average, on the part of his advisors.[23] If England had been spared despotism it was only because of the defects, not the virtues, of the men in power. But Bentham feared the situation was getting worse. The Napoleonic Wars had allowed the King and his ministers to encroach on the one important check which had previously existed against the abuse of influence. In 1795, Bentham, in considering the consequences of the implementation of his proposal for an escheat tax, had rejected the argument that the tax would increase the influence of the King dangerously:

> As for the supposed danger to liberty and to the constitution . . ., I have looked for it a good deal and never could spy it out: liberty depends not upon the greater or less influence of the Crown with relation to the servants of the public and the representatives of the people, but on the spirit of the great body of the people itself. I see very well how this spirit should be alarmed and excited by the encrease of such influence, but I do not see how it should in any degree be weakened by it. The moment the great body of the people feel any real grievance, what should hinder their complaining of it: and were the body of the people to complain of a grievance, be it ever so quietly and humbly, what can hinder it from being redressed?[24]

That optimism had now faded. The same tyranny which had sacrificed the interests of the many to the few through the use of patronage had also used its power, under the guise of the necessity of conducting an unhampered war effort, to suppress the publication of useful truth and to propagate pernicious falsehood in the press. Newspapers were being silenced and gradually, which was much worse, being 'bought or intimidated into a state of mendacious slavery'.[25] Were the papers free, then the King's extravagancies and the mechanical respect those extravagancies got from 'the foolish admiration of the people' might be ended.[26] But the press was no longer free, and so the one last important check against despotism had been removed.

These were the thoughts Bentham expressed in 1809 as he prepared a *Catechism of Parliamentary Reform* outlining the 'ends to be aimed at on the occasion of Parliamentary Reform' and the means to attain those ends.[27] The primary end of reform was to secure 'in the highest possible degree, on the part of the members [of Parliament] . . . the several *endowments* or *elements of aptitude*, necessary to fit them for the due discharge' of their trust.[28] The endowments to be sought were appropriate probity, appropriate intellectual aptitude, and appropriate active talent.

> On each occasion, whether in speaking or delivering his vote, – on the part of a representative of the people, appropriate probity consists in his pursuing that line of conduct, which, in his own sincere opinion, being not inconsistent with the rules of morality or the law of the land, is most conducive to the general good of the whole community for which he serves; that is to say, of the whole of the British empire: – forbearing, on each occasion, at the expense either of such general good, or of his duty in any shape, either to accept, or to seek to obtain, or preserve, in any shape whatsoever, for himself, or for any person or persons particularly connected with him, any advantage whatsoever, from whatsoever hands obtainable; and in particular from those hands in which, by the very frame of the constitution, the greatest mass of the matter of temptation is necessarily and unavoidably lodged, viz. those of the King, and the other members of the executive branch of the government, – the King's Ministers.[29]

Appropriate intellectual aptitude would involve the ability to form 'a right judgment' on propositions connected with governance, and active talent the ability to introduce motions, deliver speeches, draw up reports and question witnesses who might be called before the House.[30] But rather obviously, given Bentham's analysis of the role of influence, the crucial aptitude was that of probity.

Bentham believed that the appropriate endowments for members of the House could be obtained through five means: (1) Placemen would be excluded from the House 'in the quality of *members* entitled to *vote*'; (2) Official persons, named by the King from each department of the executive, could sit in the House, without the right to vote, but with the right of speaking and making motions, 'subject at all times to restriction or interdiction by the House'; (3) Elections to the House would take place annually, and the King would have the power to call for a new election at any time; (4) Speeches made in the House would be correctly, completely and authentically taken down and regularly and promptly published; (5) Constant, punctual and universal attendance would be required of all Members of Parliament.[31] Central to the success of the entire plan was the call for annual elections. These elections would be held in districts approximately equal in size, so far as was consistent with local circumstances. Voting would be by secret ballot, and the franchise would be extended to all who had paid certain, but unspecified, taxes. It was clearly Bentham's hope that a considerable extension of the franchise would result. Indeed, he saw no reason to exclude resident aliens from the franchise, provided they had paid the qualifying taxes, and he thought that '*females* might even be admitted; and perhaps with as little impropriety or danger as they are in the election of directors for the government of the 30 or 40 millions of souls in British India'.[32] This latter suggestion brought such ridicule on the plan as a whole that in his later, more radically democratic, proposals he tended to play down the issue of women's suffrage.

In 1817 Bentham claimed that the *Catechism of Parliamentary Reform* had been submitted for publication in 1809 'to one of the time-serving daily prints, in which other papers on the same subject had already found admittance. No name was sent with it: and, the weathercock being at that time upon the turn, insertion was declined.'[33] Whether Bentham's assertion was correct is impossible to say. According to a manuscript, *The Times* was the 'time-serving daily' to which the tract was submitted.[34] It is not inconceivable that *The Times* might have declined publication merely on the basis of length, for the work ran to over 10,000 words. But it is also the case that the conduct of the war against Napoleon had taken a bad turn in 1809. Sir John Moore's army, while successful in diverting Napoleon's forces from taking Lisbon and Cadiz, had narrowly avoided capture. Moore himself was killed and the army had to be evacuated:

> On the return home of Moore's force came the real crisis of the Peninsular War as far as England was concerned, – a moral and political crisis. The discouragement was great. The British public, having expected from its new allies things beyond measure, was beyond measure disillusioned. The Spaniards had indeed failed for all purposes, military and political, except guerilla warfare, and it was not yet understood how much guerilla warfare might mean in Spain. Our own army, though victorious in battle, had been forced by overwhelming numbers to re-embark. Sir John Moore himself had written that it would no longer be possible to hold Lisbon. To pessimists, Napoleon again seemed invincible on land.[35]

Since this action took place in January of 1809, and resulted in an atmosphere hardly conducive to parliamentary reform, it is conceivable that *The Times* rejected the work for the reason Bentham later suggested. But what is certain is that, despite his belief that parliamentary reform was urgently needed, Bentham made no further effort to publish the *Catechism of Parliamentary Reform* or any other writing calling for reform until 1817, two years after the end of the Napoleonic Wars.

Although he published nothing on parliamentary reform from 1809 until 1817, he continued to write away on the subject in his characteristic manner, filling page after page with analysis and argument. During the period he expressed the fear, on more than one occasion, that unless reform was instituted soon the choice facing the nation would be between accepting the despotism of the King and his ministers or embracing civil strife and revolutionary activity.[36] Bentham, though now a radical, was no revolutionary and the option, therefore, was not in his eyes a very happy one. Yet despite such fears, he himself temporised. It is possible, although it seems unlikely, that he feared that he might be prosecuted for publishing his views. By the time he did enter the lists in 1817, the repression of the press was worse than it had been in earlier years yet, for example, Bentham ignored the warnings of Sir Samuel Romilly that he was courting danger and proceeded with the publication of his views on the Church of England.[37] However one accounts for his long delay in launching a public call for reform, one point stands out. He was once again faced with a dilemma similar to that which he had faced in his early years as a reformer of the penal law, a dilemma connected with the practical problem as to how reform might actually be achieved.

Reform demanded a considerable extension of the franchise, one which would make the House of Commons dependent on the people and the government dependent on the Commons. One could hardly expect such reform to be initiated by the King or the aristocracy. Nor would support for reform be spontaneously generated in the House of Commons itself. Reform would mean a considerable sacrifice of the Members' existing interests. It would mean the end to sinecures and places for themselves and for their friends and relatives. It would mean a loss of power to borough holders and opulent country gentlemen. It would mean that the Members in general would actually have to attend the sessions of Parliament and to work at their legislative duties, something which was not required of them under existing conditions. These and other sacrifices were hardly to be expected without their being some motive to reform, and the mere fact that the reforms would benefit the people at large could hardly be a sufficient motive given the strength of the selfish interest in any given Member of Parliament and the weakness of the social interest. It would be the height of folly and absurdity to believe that they would easily give up their property in corruption.[38]

The only chance for success depended on the degree of uneasiness produced in the minds of the Members of Parliament. They must be made aware that the degree of discontent with the existing situation was widespread and strongly felt, and this could be done basically in two ways: through public rallies and petitions. It is clear Bentham had some reservations about the utility of public rallies. He was aware that the apparent tumultuousness of such assemblies had been used to argue that the people were not fit to govern, that they were unwilling to listen to both sides of an argument. Nevertheless Bentham tried to show that in the past as in the present, such rallies took place only when the instances of misconduct upon the part of the governors were numerous and obvious; and that they had succeeded, on occasion, in heading off what was later recognised as a growing despotism. The present issue was a great one, a contest between corruption and in-corruption, a test to see whether the government, which had been growing worse and worse, would be restored to integrity and brought in line with the improvements which had occurred within the society itself. Public disturbances were not produced by democracy but, rather, by the want of it.[39] But despite this support for public demonstrations, Bentham also held that the only legal and constitutional method of bringing about reform was to petition the Parliament and the King. To be successful, such petitions could not be made too frequently nor could they be other than troublesome to the House of Commons. Bentham knew that great difficulties stood in the way of success, and, for that reason, called for unity and co-operation among all reformers as well as openness in admitting that reform would mean the sacrifice of existing interests.[40]

Bentham was aware that there were those who opposed reform because they feared initiating a course of events similar to what had happened in France after 1789. He believed that some who took this line were simply masking their sinister interests, but others were sincere. Accordingly Bentham sought to distinguish the French situation from that in England. Not the least evil of the French Revolution was the emotional check it had created against the reasonable discussion of reasonable reform. But it was a fallacy to draw arguments from France and apply them to England. The temper of the French people was, and ever had been, more brisk and irritable than that of the English. At the time of the Revolution, the bulk of the people in France had been in a state of almost universal ignorance about everything that concerned government. There had been no popular assemblies of any kind. There were no newspapers or political pamphleteers to inform them. In

England, by contrast, there was a long tradition of newspapers and political writers informing the public. Although that very tradition was now threatened, the people still were far better informed than the French people. The English were not given to protesting for 'light and transcient causes'.[41] A more relevant example for England was what had happened and was happening in the United States of America. There one could find 'a set of *minds* – minds sprung from our own', hence nearer to the English in a 'psychological sense'.[42] Yet though that country was born in revolution, nevertheless a stable and successful government had been established, one which was free from anarchy and posed no threat to property.

But Bentham was quick to add that he did not intend that England be democratised like America. He was simply trying to show the incorrectness of the argument that democracy leads to anarchy. The English people had no desire to take all power from the Crown. They had demonstrated abiding patience with the King despite considerable provocation:

> Continuing in such tranquility under all these provocations always without a thought of making any change in the government – always loving it, always praising it, always priding themselves on it, is there any the smallest chance that by the removal of any or all of these past causes of discontent their attachment to the government should be lessened, any desire to overthrow it generated?[43]

But, as this remark suggests, therein lay the problem for Bentham. If the patience of the people, their peacefulness and passivity in the face of abuse, could be used as an argument to show that it would not be dangerous to extend the franchise to them, it also made Bentham wonder whether or not they would, through petition and protest, rally sufficiently to the cause of reform. General interest in reform was weak among the public both because public-spiritedness itself was weak, and because the particular impact of corruption on the self-interest of any one citizen was not great even though the total mass of corruption was enormous and growing every day.[44] How, then, was reform to be won?

By 1817, Bentham's grievances against the government had grown. He was convinced that the Church of England had only established the National School Society in order to thwart the efforts of Joseph Lancaster and others, including Bentham himself, to establish either nonconformist or nonsectarian schools. In Bentham's eyes this was but another attempt to keep the people in subservient blindness to the corruption so rife within the Church and the State. Reticent for so long about making his views about the Church known, he sought to publish an attack on the Church in 1817 under the pseudonym 'Oxford

Graduate', in the hope that he would not alienate those members of the Church who supported parliamentary reform. He was thwarted in this effort because the government of the day was punishing publishers and booksellers of anonymous works which it considered to be libellous or blasphemous. Thus, in 1818, Bentham added his name to a new title page and published *Church-of-Englandism and its Catechism examined* which included an attack on the National School Society:

> *Mendacity* and *insincerity* – in these I found, . . . the effects – the sure and only sure effects – of an English University education: of a Church of England education of the first quality: these, sooner or later, I could not but see in the number, not only of its *effects*, but of its *objects*: of mendacity, a forced *act* or two: and the object of it the securing of an *habit* of insincerity throughout life.
>
> Another thing, which I moreover beheld most certainly among the effects, and but too probably among the objects, of Church of England doctrine, enforced by Church of England discipline, was, – that 'humble docility' as towards its rulers and their subordinates – that 'prostration of the understanding and will', which, in so many words, with an intrepidity that cannot sufficiently be admired, the *Bishop of London*, on a late *Charge*, . . ., has published as the avowed object of their endeavours: their *National Society's* Schools, and this their Catechism, being employed as instruments to this purpose.[45]

A public educated under the tutelage of the Church of England would be worse than a public not educated at all, for it would mean learned ignorance, obsequious and subservient behaviour. If the Church were to have her way, all chance for reform would soon be lost.

Nor was it only the activity of the Church of England which deepened Bentham's sense of concern. Although the Napoleonic Wars were over, the English garrisoned some 50,000 troops in France. Although the presence of the troops had been defended in the name of security, in Bentham's eyes the purpose was to subvert the liberties of the French and to put the French people in subjection. But what could be done today to the French with a standing army of such size could happen to England tomorrow:

> The plains, or heights, or whatsoever they are, of *Waterloo* – will one day be pointed to by the historian as the grave – not only of French, but of English liberties. Not of France alone, but of Britain with her, was the conquest consummated in the Netherlands. Whatsoever has been done and is doing in France, will soon be done in Britain. Reader, would you wish to know the lot designed for you? Look to France, there you may behold it.[46]

Bentham's fears may have been exaggerated. But it was not Bentham alone who believed that the spectre of Napoleon had been replaced by an even greater threat. As Shelley wrote in the *Feelings of a Republican on the Fall of Bonaparte:*

> I hated thee, fallen tyrant! I did groan
> To think that a most unambitious slave,
> Like thou, shouldst dance and revel on the grave
> Of Liberty. Thou mightst have built thy throne
> Where it had stood even now: thou didst prefer
> A frail and bloody pomp which Time has swept
> In fragments towards Oblivion. Massacre,
> For this I prayed, would on thy sleep have crept,
> Treason and Slavery, Rapine, Fear, and Lust,
> And stifled thee, their minister. I know
> Too late, since thou and France are in the dust,
> That Virtue owns a more eternal foe
> Than Force or Fraud: old Custom, legal Crime,
> And bloody Faith the foulest birth of Time.[47]

For the singularly unpoetic Bentham, it was precisely 'old Custom, legal Crime, and bloody Faith' backed up by 'Force' and 'Fraud' which were bringing England to the brink of ruin. Thus it was that finally, in 1817, Bentham began the public campaign for reform which was to occupy him until the day of his death in 1832, on the eve of the passage of the great Reform Bill.

Upon finally publishing the *Catechism of Parliamentary Reform*, Bentham added an Introduction almost eight times the length of the original work. Although his grievances and his fears had deepened, he still had not reached the point of completely rejecting the English form of government. But the tone of the Introduction is acerbic in contrast to that of the generally dispassionate *Catechism*. In the original work, he admitted 'that even the worst king and the worst minister having, on many points, the same interest with the body of the people, it is not in the nature of man, that they should harbour any such intention, or any such wish, as that of doing, on any occasion any act, that may be in any degree productive of injury to the general interest, except in so far as it may happen to this or that particular interest of their own to be served by such act.' Thus so long 'as they content themselves with doing no other sort of mischief than what has been commonly done already, – they stand assured of support, not only from each other, but from the multitude'.[48] In contrast, there are dire warnings and threats in the 'Introduction': 'Drawn on, in the road to that gulf, from those times down to the present, – the country, if my eyes do not deceive me, is already at the very brink: – reform or convulsion, such is the alternative',[49] Nor is much benefit of the doubt given to the possibility of the 'worst king' and the 'worst minister' having much in common with the great body of the people:

> Gagging Bills – suspension of the Habeas Corpus Act – interdiction of all communication between man and man for any such purpose as that of complaint or remedy – all these have already become precedent – all these are in preparation – all these are regarded as things of course.
>
> The pit is already dug: one after another, or all together, the securities called *English liberties* will be cast into it.[50]

In addition, exorbitant taxation and a reckless fiscal policy lay heavy upon the great mass of the people, and why? Simply to support the desire for money, power and factitious dignity upon the part of the King, his ministers and the aristocracy:

> Such is the state in which the country lies: – the universal interest crouching under the conjunct yoke of two partial and adverse interests, to which, to a greater or less extent, it ever has been made, – and to the greatest extent possible, as far as depends upon them, cannot, in the nature of man and things, ever cease to be made, a continual sacrifice.
>
> For the consummation of this sacrifice, adequate *inclination* – such is the nature of man – never could have been wanting: – but as to the *power* – the effective power – never at any former period could it have been seen swelled to a pitch approaching to that at which it stands at this present moment.[51]

Despite these feelings, Bentham did not call for the extirpation of the monarchy and the House of Lords. All that was needed was the establishment of democratic ascendancy.

Democratic ascendancy would be a sufficient check against the threats to liberty and the practices of corruption. The Introduction did entertain broadening the franchise in some respects over that proposed in the *Catechism*. Although Bentham now felt that to decide on the issue of female suffrage was 'altogether premature', he also felt that to restrict the franchise to householders was dubious. He himself recognised the bewilderment and fear which might be caused in others at the suggestion of universal manhood suffrage:

> Such, at any rate in my own view, it cannot fail to be: for in this state, for a long course of years, was my own mind: – the object a dark, and thence a hideous phantom, until, elicited by severe and

> external pressure, the light of *reason* – or, if this word be too assuming, the light of *ratiocination* – was brought to bear upon it. In the *Plan* itself may be seen at what period (viz. anno 1809,) fearful of going further – embracing the occasion of finding, in *derivative* judgment, an exterior support – I was not only content, but glad, to stop at the degree of extension indicated by the word *householders;* – taking at the same time for conclusive evidence of *householdership*, the fact of having paid *direct taxes*.[52]

But the more he had applied his mind to the subject the more he became convinced that there was no danger in virtual universal suffrage. Any exceptions to that practice would have to be justified with sound reasons, showing how the exception was in the interests of the greatest happiness of the greatest number. The interests of all, whether householders or not, were affected by the actions of government even in regard to taxation; nor was everything the government did a matter of taxation. Direct taxes on householders fell indirectly on those who paid rents to inhabit their houses, so that a rise in the rates affected both parties. If wealth in the form of property was thought to be a check against irresponsible electoral demands, was it a superior check to wealth of other kinds? Was it not the case that those who rented rooms from householders were, on occasion, wealthier than the householder? Was it not the case that where virtual universal suffrage already existed, as within the borough of Westminster, there was no evidence whatsoever to suggest that the propertyless classes had in any way abused their trust?[53]

Bentham was now a public proponent of democratic ascendancy. But he was anxious to associate his ideas, so far as possible, with the respectable proponents of democracy. He castigated and mocked Cobbett, and linked his own proposals with the argument made in earlier years by the Duke of Richmond and Charles Fox that the establishment of democratic ascendancy through manhood suffrage would not be an innovation but a restoration of the traditional rights of Englishmen.[54] But in the succeeding years, Bentham became ever more uncompromising in his support of democracy, ever more radical in his demands. In the *Constitutional Code*, which has been described as a presentation of Bentham's 'ideal republic',[55] he was no longer open to the idea that much of the English Constitution ought to remain intact:

> To the whole contents of this proposed code, one all-comprehensive objection will not fail to be opposed. In whatever political community, by which it were adopted, it would, to a greater or less extent, probably to a very large extent, involve the abolition of existing institutions.
>
> But, by whomsoever this unquestionable truth is put forward in

> the character of an objection, let it be understood what the confession is which is involved in it. It is, – that among the institutions, to which the objector is thus giving his support, there exist in an indefinite number, those, of the mischievousness of which he is himself fully conscious, – that, in what he is thus endeavouring at, he therefore acts, to his own full knowledge, the part of an enemy to the community to which he belongs, and for whose welfare he pretends to be solicitous.[56]

Apparently there could be no honest, if mistaken, opposition to Bentham's design for a government, nor any erroneous conceptualisation in his own plan. The same Bentham who had criticised the French Declaration of the Rights of Man for holding that 'every authority is usurped and void, to which a man has been appointed in any other mode than that of popular election'[57] ended his career by claiming that only a representative democracy could and would actually pursue the greatest happiness of the greatest number; and that representative democracy could and would best do so by approximating or actually adopting the form of government set out in the *Constitutional Code*. If Bentham had been remarkably flexible and undogmatic for the better part of his life, the last fifteen years were marked by a growing inflexibility and dogmatism, characteristics matched by the increasing tendency to treat his personal associates with vituperation and scorn. Yet Bentham, though an angry old man, was not insane, and if his prose in these later years lacked lucidity, his ideas, however wrong they might be, did not.

Notes Chapter IV

1 Alexander Pope, *An Essay on Man*, Epistle III, 11, 303–4.
2 Elie Halévy, *The Growth of Philosophic Radicalism*, trans. Mary Morris (Boston, Mass., The Beacon Press, 1955), p. 254.
3 *Works*, IV, p. 39 (*Panopticon, or The Inspection House*).
4 ibid., pp. 3–33 (*A View of the Hard-Labour Bill*).
5 *Works*, XI, p. 97.
6 ibid., p. 98.
7 See Samuel's criticisms, particularly directed at *A View of the Hard-Labour Bill*, in his letter to Jeremy (2–13 August 1782), *Correspondence*, III, pp. 136–7.
8 *Works*, IV, pp. 47, 49–50, 58, 79–86, 122 (*Panopticon, . . .*) and pp. 174, 242–5 (*Panopticon versus New South Wales*).
9 *Works*, IV, p. 37 (title page) and pp. 60–6 (*Panopticon, . . .*).
10 ibid., pp. 173–284.
11 ibid., pp. 252–3, 261 (*A Plea for the Constitution*).

12 *Works*, x, p. 201.
13 ibid., pp. 201, 212. Bowring reprints the 'Anti-Machiavel' letters at ibid., pp. 201–11.
14 ibid., p. 212.
15 Halévy, op. cit., pp. 251–61. Halévy, it should be noted, does add some qualifications to the theory that Bentham became a democrat as a result of his frustrations over Panopticon although others, following his emphasis, have not been so cautious.
16 Gertrude Himmelfarb, 'The Haunted House of Jeremy Bentham', *Victorian Minds* (New York, Harper Torchbooks, 1970), p. 71, n. 9. See also Mary Mack, *Jeremy Bentham: An Odyssey of Ideas 1748–1792* (London, Heinemann, 1962), pp. 400–1 and Bentham's 'History of the War between Jeremy Bentham and George III', Additional Manuscripts of the British Museum 33, 530, pp. 365–416, which is partially printed in *Works*, XI, pp. 96–105.
17 UC 127, p. 20. On the relationship of motives to the moral consequences of actions, see *IPML*, pp. 96–142 where Bentham distinguishes between 'motives' and 'dispositions'.
18 *Works*, VI, p. 246 (*Rational of Judicial Evidence*).
19 ibid.
20 UC 126, pp. 19–21, 23, 26–7, 32, 42, 48–50, 79–80, 171, 205–7, 210, 300–40; UC 125, pp. 27–9.
21 UC 126, pp. 346–7. See also UC 126, pp. 272–87.
22 UC 126, pp. 98–100.
23 UC 128, p. 123; UC 126, p. 384.
24 *Economic Writings*, I, p. 339 (*Supply without Burthen*).
25 UC 126, p. 57. Also UC 126, pp. 48, 393–4 and UC 128, p. 123. See Arthur Aspinall, *Politics and the Press c. 1750–1850* (London, Home & Van Thal, 1949), pp. 33–5, 39–41.
26 UC 129, pp. 55–6.
27 *Works*, III, p. 539 (*Catechism of Parliamentary Reform*).
28 ibid.
29 ibid.
30 ibid., pp. 539–40.
31 ibid., p. 540.
32 ibid., pp. 540–1.
33 ibid., p. 435 (Introduction to the *Catechism of Parliamentary Reform*).
34 UC 125, p. 184.
35 G. M. Trevelyan, *British History in the Nineteenth Century and After: 1782–1919* (New York, Harper Torchbooks, 1966), p. 124.
36 UC 125, p. 128; UC 128, pp. 120–30; UC 129, p. 341.
37 *The Life of Sir Samuel Romilly, with a Selection from His Correspondence*, 3rd edn, 2 vols (London, John Murray, 1842), vol. II, pp. 489–90. See also Aspinall, op. cit., 39–44, 50–1.
38 UC 125, pp. 126–7, 132; UC 127, pp. 107–14.
39 UC 127, pp. 27–47.
40 UC 127, pp. 75, 78–101.
41 UC 127, pp. 35–40, 47. The quotation, of course, is from the United States Declaration of Independence, out of John Locke's *Second Treatise of Government*, ch. XIX, paras 223–5.
42 UC 127, p. 41; UC 129, p. 72.
43 UC 126, p. 413. See also UC 126, pp. 409–12 and UC 127, pp. 42–4.

44 *Works*, III, p. 445 (Introduction to the *Catechism of Parliamentary Reform*); UC 127, pp. 107–14.

45 *Church-of-Englandism and its Catechism examined* (London, Effingham Wilson, 1818), 'Preface', pp. xxi–xxii. Bentham's reference to the Bishop of London is to William Howley, *A Charge delivered to the Clergy of the Diocese of London* (London, T. Bensley, 1814), especially p. 16. An account of the difficulties Bentham met in publishing his attack may be found in the papers bound with Sir Francis Place's copy of *Church-of-Englandism* in the British Library.

46 *Works*, III, p. 436 and pp. 436–8 in general (Introduction to the *Catechism of Parliamentary Reform*).

47 Percy Shelley, *Poetical Works*, ed. Thomas Hutchinson, a new edition corrected by G. M. Matthews (London, Oxford University Press, 1970), pp. 526–7.

48 *Works*, III, p. 542 (*Catechism* . . .).

49 ibid., p. 435 (Introduction . . .).

50 ibid.

51 ibid., p. 440.

52 ibid., p. 467 n., and p. 463.

53 ibid., pp. 465–76.

54 ibid., pp. 469, 471, 475–6, 480–1 n. See also the *Sketch of the Various Proposals for a Constitutional Reform* which Bentham added as an appendix to a subsequent printing of the *Catechism*, pp. 553–7.

55 Thomas P. Peardon, 'Bentham's Ideal Republic', *Canadian Journal of Economics & Political Science*, XVII (May 1951), pp. 184–203.

56 *Works*, IX, p. 1 (*Constitutional Code*).

57 *Works*, II, p. 505 (*Anarchical Fallacies*).

Chapter V

A Tyranny of the Majority?

In his later years Bentham was no longer content with mere democratic ascendancy. By the time he wrote the *Constitutional Code*, he had concluded that the 'axiom' that 'in the general tenor of life, in every human breast, self-regarding interest is predominant over all other interests put together', meant that any ruler not subjected to control would on all occasions prefer his own interest to the interests of the people.[1] The only form of government which could provide adequate checks to prevent this from happening was a pure representative democracy. A mixed form of government, even with democratic ascendancy, would leave far too much room for the corruption of the people's representatives and result in the exploitation of the people. Governmental power must be concentrated in the hands of a popularly elected unitary legislature, so that there would be no doubt as to where responsibility rested for governmental misrule. Thus, although the United States of America had served Bentham as the primary proof of the undangerousness of democracy and as the leading example of a government actually seeking the greatest happiness of the greatest number, the Constitution of the United States was not the model for Bentham's ideal republic. There were too many elements in that Constitution, including the bicameral legislature, which impeded popular control, made the system too complicated and provided too much room for abuse. A bicameral system was unnecessary and dangerous. A hereditary second house or one appointed by anyone other than the people themselves would be undemocratic and was simply out of the question. An elected second house would be either superfluous or undemocratic. If it was elected on the only defensible plan of popular suffrage in relatively equal districts, it would be superfluous for it would simply reproduce the pattern of representation found in the other house. To employ any other mode of election would mean that the house was undemocratic, and hence dangerous. It would mean that those representing a minority of the people might be able to block the will of those representing a majority, and there should be no such impediment to the will of the majority.[2]

In a properly constituted democracy, the people should not only elect their representatives annually by secret ballot, but a majority of the electors in any district should be able to recall their representative at any time and even to bring legal charges against him. Nor were the powers of the 'supreme constitutive assembly' to end there. Since there was always the danger of collusion between the representative and the administrative branch of government, it was necessary that the people be given the power to institute the process by which members of the administration, including the prime minister, might be removed from office.[3] The voters as a whole, then, were to be supreme, either directly or indirectly, in locating or dislocating the government, both in the legislative and the administrative branches. That supremacy, subject to revocation, would be given over to the legislature once it was constituted. There were to be no restraints on what the legislature might do, no independent executive with a power of veto, no bill of rights, no judiciary with the right to declare a law unconstitutional: 'The Supreme Legislature is omnicompetent. Coexistence with the territory of the state is its local field of service; coextensive with the field of human action is its logical field of service. – To its power, there are no limits.'[4] So long as the legislature maintained the support of a majority of the voters in the country, it could enact any law it thought fit. Moreover, it was given considerable power to see to it that the laws, once enacted, were properly administered according to the intentions of the legislative body:

> The Supreme Legislative Authority has, for its immediate instrument, the Supreme *Executive*, composed of the *administrative* and the *judiciary*, acting within their respective spheres. On the will of the Supreme Constitutive the Supreme Legislative is dependent, . . . Absolute and all-comprehensive is this dependence. So also, on the will of the Legislature the will of the Executive, and the wills of the Sub-legislatures.[5]

The administrative branch of government would be headed by a prime minister chosen by the legislature for a four-year term of office, and only eligible for re-election at such a time as 'there are in existence, at the same time, out of whom choice may be made' two or three former prime ministers.[6] Bentham particularly stressed the appropriate term for the office: '*Minister* is from the Latin, and means *servant*. All functionaries belonging to the Administrative are, as such, *servants* – located and dislocable servants – of the *Legislature*.'[7] The prime minister was not to be a political leader, for he was subordinate to the legislature. Nor was he to be a 'President' for he was not to preside over the legislature.

Indeed, he was permitted to attend legislative sessions only upon the invitation of the legislature. He could, however, address the legislature via written messages of three types: (1) he could provide information to them; (2) he could make general suggestions of subject matters for consideration by them; (3) he could propose ordinances, *in terminis*, which he thought suitable for enactment.[8]

The administrative branch of government, ideally, was to be made up of career civil servants with special expertise in the area of their ministry. The ministers heading the thirteen departments Bentham recommended would be selected by the prime minister. In principle he could select anyone he might like. But Bentham hoped that, in practice, he would be ill-advised to select anyone other than one of the leading candidates proposed to him by a specially constituted examination or qualification judicatory. This body would appraise the skills and rank the various candidates for office and, presumably, its attention would be focused on the senior civil servants within any department. Having evaluated the candidates, it would then conduct that most curious of Benthamic devices, a 'patriotic auction' wherein the candidates would specify the pay for which they were willing to work or, indeed, the amount they would be willing to pay to hold the office. Talents being more or less equal, it was presumed that the prime minister would select the candidate who would work for the least amount of money. Once in office, a minister's term was for life, revocable with cause by the prime minister and with or without cause by the legislature or at the initiative of the people.[9]

It is impossible to give a summary of the major features of Bentham's ideal republic which would be brief yet adequate.[10] But the main principles on which all of his recommendations were based are easily summarised: maximise aptitude in government while minimising expense; minimise public confidence in the legislature and administration alike, while maximising public distrust and suspicion of all official persons. Public opinion must be provided with every possible channel to make its voice heard. The public must be provided with the greatest number of controls to prevent any misrule by the governors.

For John Stuart Mill, these principles would have led to the establishment of a tyranny of the unthinking majority over all minority groups and, in particular, over men of intelligence and ability. Indeed, Mill feared that Benthamic principles were already contributing to the growing tyranny of the majority even though few, if any, of the democratic institutions Bentham had proposed on the basis of those principles had been adopted. Bentham's narrowness had led him to concern himself only with the question of how to prevent abuses of governmental authority:

> That extraordinary power which he posessed, of at once seizing comprehensive principles, and scheming out minute details, is brought into play with surpassing vigour in devising means for preventing rulers from escaping from the control of the majority; for enabling and inducing the majority to exercise that control unremittingly; and for providing them with servants of every desirable endowment, moral and intellectual, compatible with entire subservience to their will.[11]

But a majority which could control government in order to prevent misrule could also cause that government to act in ways detrimental to others than the majority itself. Mill doubted whether, in fact, it was good for mankind to be placed under 'the absolute authority of the majority of themselves'.[12]

> We say the authority, not the political authority merely, because it is chimerical to suppose that whatever has absolute power over men's bodies will not arrogate it over their minds – will not seek to control (not perhaps by legal penalties, but by the persecutions of society) opinions and feelings which depart from its standard; will not attempt to shape the education of the young by its model, and to extinguish all books, all schools, all combinations of individuals for joint action upon society, which may be attempted for the purpose of keeping alive a spirit at variance with its own. Is it, we say, the proper condition of man, in all ages and nations, to be under the despotism of Public Opinion?[13]

Mill's answer was based on his estimate of the character of the majority in any society, even the most advanced one:

> The numerical majority of any society whatever, must consist of persons all standing in the same social position, and having, in the main, the same pursuits, namely, unskilled manual labourers; and we mean no disparagement to them: whatever we say to their disadvantage, we say equally of a numerical majority of shopkeepers, or of squires. Where there is identity of position and pursuits, there also will be identity of partialities, passions, and prejudices; and to give any set of partialities, passions, and prejudices, absolute power, without counter-balance from partialities, passions, and prejudices of a different sort, is the way to render the correction of any of those imperfections hopeless; to make one narrow, mean type of human nature universal and perpetual, and to crush every influence which tends to the further improvement of man's intellectual and moral nature.[14]

Bentham had overlooked the necessity of providing for freedom of thought and individuality of character and in his concern to provide against misrule by the governors he had forgotten to provide against misrule by the majority of the people.

In fact, Bentham himself had expressed sentiments similar to Mill's about the 'clamorous and unruly multitude'.[15] Particularly at the height of his reaction to the French Revolution he had gone far beyond Mill in deploring those who were willing to trust the 'unthinking multitude':

> What, then, shall we say of that system of government, of which the professed object is to call upon the untaught and unlettered multitude (whose existence depends upon their devoting their whole time to the acquisition of the means of supporting it,) to occupy themselves without ceasing upon all questions of government (legislation and administration included) without exception – important and trivial, – the most general and the most particular, but more especially upon the most important and most general – that is, in other words, the most scientific – those that require the greatest measures of science to qualify a man for deciding upon, and in respect of which any want of science and skill are liable to be attended with the most fatal consequences?[16]

To believe that such questions of government could be answered by the people was comparable to believing that the great questions of chemistry should be answered by primary assemblies rather than by the French Academy of Science.

Nor were Bentham's arguments against democracy restricted to the untutored French in contrast with his own countrymen. Everywhere and at all times, the great majority of men would have to spend the better part of their lives earning enough to survive. As a consequence, they simply could not devote the necessary time to the difficult questions of government. Bentham rejected the notion that it was unnecessary for the people to be fully informed on such subjects, that all that was required was competence to select representatives who would decide on what should be done by the government: 'To choose men he must be able to judge them[;] to judge them he must judge their measures – to judge their measures he must understand what are the measures that in every case ought to have been adopted.' To do this 'every man must be equal to the whole business of government'.[17] But to believe that was possible was absurd. There were few men of education equal to the whole business of government. An entire life employed in nothing else but the study of legislation would not be enough time to acquire such learning. Nor was it merely a matter of time. A variety of prejudices must be overcome before one can see the issues of government with clarity. But the great bulk of men have their minds closed by prejudices which are deep-seated and most difficult to root out. The majority of men respond to sounds, not to sense, and to establish their hegemony would be to establish the rule of the ill-inforned over that of the informed classes. In fact, as a result of the rule of the ignorant, democratic governments have always been characterised by ignorance, violence, extravagence, discontent and frequent wars.[18]

Upon becoming a democrat, then, Bentham seems to have drastically altered his judgement about the great body of men. In contrast to his earlier views, he now maintained that 'in the labouring – the productive class, life in its general tenor, is a life of beneficence: whatever maleficence has place forms the exception, and in comparison with the beneficence, those exceptions are extremely rare'.[19] He still argued that the people were not capable of actually conducting the legislative, administrative or judicial work of government. But he now held that they, and they alone, were qualified to choose their legislators. 'Considered by itself and without reference to any other, this greatest number, say, for shortness, *the people*, cannot on any just grounds be considered as deficient, in respect of aggregate appropriate aptitude.'[20] In respect to moral aptitude, the ability of the people was at a maximum:

> Not only does the moral aptitude of the people dispose them to look out for, and choose morally apt agents; but it disposes all men who are, or who wish to be such agents, to become morally apt. The only interest of his, which an elector can expect to serve by the choice of an agent for this purpose, is that which he has in common with all the rest. The only way in which, in quality of agent for this purpose, a man can expect to recommend himself to the good opinion and choice of the people in their quality of electors, is by appearing disposed to serve to his utmost this practically universal interest: and the only sure way of appearing disposed to serve it, is to be actually conspicuous in his endeavours to serve it.[21]

The people would be able to see through attempted deception. They would not only be disposed to choose morally apt agents but they would also have sufficient intellectual aptitude to make this choice, in the aggregate, a correct one. Thus they would choose representatives who were not only dedicated to pursuing the greatest happiness of the greatest number, but who were intelligent and active enough to succeed in that pursuit.

Given the general beneficence of the people, they would scarcely expect their representatives to pursue the greatest happiness of the greatest number at the expense of any minority (except those of the obviously criminal class). Thus the problem of majority tyranny appears to have been no problem at all for Bentham by the time he became a democrat. Hence the structure of government proposed in the *Constitutional Code* was almost a matter of course, particularly since many of the elements had been embraced by Bentham long before he became a democrat. He had consistently questioned the utility of a bill of rights, as is shown by his attack on the French Declaration of the Rights of Man during his most conservative of moods. His attack on the common law was directed against judge-made law and, hence, precluded him from accepting the American doctrine of judicial review. And from the beginning of his career he had doubted the effectiveness and necessity of a bicameral system. Even at the height of his reaction to the French Revolution, his defence of the English House of Lords was, at best, half-hearted.[22]

It might seem then, that, convinced of the undangerousness of the people, Bentham was now simply showing the courage of convictions which he had held for many years. This is certainly part of the story, but only part of it. For even after he became a democrat, Bentham continued, on occasion, to express concern over the aptitude of the people. In the *Constitutional Code* itself, Bentham deplored 'the stupid ignorant patience of the people' who so willingly tolerated the corruption and misrule by the King, 'the arch-depredator'; and he could write of 'the undiscerning and unscrutinizing multitude' who so readily believed that the praise bestowed on 'the powerful, the dignified, and the wealthy' by toadies (and, in particular, by poets) was, in itself, 'conclusive evidence of merit, virtue, excellence' when, in fact, no such qualities existed in the recipients of the praise.[23] He felt that the 'aristocratical' section of the population had a considerable advantage over the 'democratical':

> In the aristocratical section is the acknowledged standard of taste; and the taste of the aristocrat is always conformable to, and to a great extent determined by, interest – by their separate and sinister interest. To increase their own importance, the ambitious youth of the democratical section, and those who float between the two sections, make a point of adopting declaredly the tastes and opinions of the aristocratical, that they may be regarded as belonging to it, and be accordingly respected and courted.
>
> By substituting the principle of taste to the greatest happiness principle, taste is made the arbiter of excellence and depravity; and thus the great mass of the community is in the very sink of depravity. Witness the use that is made of the words *bad taste* and *disgusting*. Bad taste pours down contempt: disgusting is a superlative above flagitious, – it is a *quasi* conjugate of *taste* and *bad taste*. Those of the

democratical section, in so far as they adopt such expressions, act in support of the hostile section against themselves. For the rich and powerful will always be the arbiters of taste: what is an object of disgust to them will, to those who follow this principle, be an object of disgust likewise.[24]

In respect to matters of taste, Bentham held, in particular, that there were certain subjects on which the force of public opinion was determined by 'sinister impulse' rather than concern for the greatest happiness of the greatest number. Thus, because of the foolish regard the majority had for showing gratitude for favours received, they not only tolerated but approved of the obsequiousness shown by those corrupted by the King even though obsequiousness and corruption were injurious to the interests of the majority.[25] Moreover, because of a 'want of sufficient maturity in the public judgment, the popular antipathy has been drawn upon this or that act, the nature of which is not, upon the balance, of a pernicious nature'. As a consequence certain minorities suffered unnecessary unhappiness because of defamatory opinions held by the majority. Such cases included instances where 'the public mind is infected with the disease of intolerance in matters of religion'; 'the field of taste' where 'eccentricity of any veneral appetite, the sexual for example', is reprobated even though no pain, and hence no evil, is caused anyone; and the harm done by revealing 'a breach of a marriage contract, on either side, more particularly the female'.[26] In such cases, whether public opinion acted through the moral or the political sanction, unnecessary harm was done to individuals and there was a diminution of the greatest happiness of the greatest number. Indeed, one might well say that the majority acted tyrannically toward a minority.

In order to understand why, despite such views, Bentham was not particularly concerned about majority tyranny, one must keep in mind that, while he was proposing the *Constitutional Code* as a model for all nations, he did not think it likely that his suggestions would be accepted even in England for some time to come. The significance of that belief must be measured by the fact that, even when he became hostile toward the King and the English Government, he could admit that the English form of government had been, until the advent of what he called the Anglo-American United States, the government which most approximated the goal of pursuing the greatest happiness of the greatest number. In fact, in many respects, it was still the least bad government among all those which were not representative democracies, although surely in grave danger of losing that claim to limited approval.[27] The government proposed in the *Constitutional Code* was a model for the future and, as he had written many years before, a model approaching perfection was of utility even if its adoption was a distant possibility, since it could serve as a guide for successive approximations.[28]

A model which could only work on the condition of a radical transformation of human nature was of no utility. Bentham did not believe he had made any such supposition and, in fact, thought that there was evidence to show that a plan on the order of that proposed in the *Constitutional Code* would work. After all, an approximation to it, however imperfect, had already taken place in the United States as a whole as well as within the individual states which made up the union. The experience of the United States convinced Bentham that there was a growing coincidence between public opinion and the dictates of the greatest happiness principle. Since he still believed that the unequal distribution of property was necessary for there to be economic growth and, as a result, abundance, he was pleased to find that in the United States the respect for private property was shared by a vast portion of the population. In earlier years he had maintained that it was foolish to attempt to equalise property because it was, in fact, impossible to do so; yet he feared that the majority, i.e. the poor, might nevertheless embrace such a foolish policy.[29] In his later years, his argument appears to be that since the policy was foolish, the majority would never adopt it:

> If therefore all persons capable of exercising a share in supreme power had all of them a share in it no such consequence [as equality of possessions] would ensure. Universal community of possessions would in their eyes be universal slavery: nor could they be so blind as not to see that howsoever the case might be in regard to equality of the shares in the supreme power, as to such possessions of which the matter of subsistence and opulence is conferred, any equalization incompatible with security would be equalization but in name & destruction – immediate destruction – in effect.[30]

Thus, in one important area where majority tyranny might be expected, there was no cause for concern. The majority itself recognised that to seize the property of the rich would be detrimental to all, minority and majority alike.

More generally, Bentham held that most, if not all, topics where public opinion and the dictates of the greatest happiness principle were in conflict were topics where the public mind had been deluded by holders of offices which would no longer exist under the plan of the *Constitutional Code* and which did not exist in the United States. King, Lords and Established Church would be eliminated, and with their elimination there would be an end to the worst sources of delusion. If corruption was principally used to cause the representatives of the people to betray their trust, 'the class of persons on whom the most important effects of delusive influence are performed, are the people themselves'.[31]

> The instruments by which delusion may be produced, in company with corruption, are principally of that sort which operate by some special association which they have with the condition of the great pampered ruler: of this sort are the trappings of monarchy: fruits or indications of the matchless opulence so constantly attached to supreme power when placed in a single hand: the gorgeous palaces, the glittering throne, and still more glittering crown. Only as examples can these elements serve; for the multitude and variety of them is inexhaustible.
>
> The objects of delusion are, to cause men to take an improper end for the proper end of government: and to entertain erroneous conceptions respecting the dispositions of the persons exercising the powers of government.[32]

If such instruments of delusion had worked all too well in most nations, they would have no place in Bentham's ideal republic. Hence the chances for the public mind being rightly informed were enormously increased. Men do desire their own greatest happiness and they have no particular desire to cause unnecessary harm to others.[33] When they fail to act rightly they do so because they have not judged correctly. Bentham never held that the axiom that each man is the best judge of his own interest meant that an individual was an infallible judge. The opinions on which the majority act would be 'in the highest degree contributory to the greatest happiness of the greatest number, in so far as the conception entertained by the several members in relation to their respective interests is correct'.[34] But that conception might be wrong. It was all too frequently wrong in existing governments both because of the instruments of delusion used to blind the people, and because such governments frequently withheld the information which would be necessary for the people to judge correctly. Such practices would cease in Bentham's ideal republic. A government subject to regular election by the voters would not dare to withhold information for long or to employ instruments of delusion. Information would be supplied to the people by the government and the press. The people, who would be better educated in a regime where adequate formal schooling was not prevented by a jealous Church and a fearful government, would have an active interest in how they were governed. Accordingly they would bestow the necessary degree of attention on the information provided and arrive at correct conclusions on the issues of the day.[35] A mass of information, then, would minimise the blindness of the majority and, consequently, maximise the greatest happiness of the greatest number.

A crucial factor in enlightening the public to its own interest and preventing it from doing unwarranted harm to minorities was the rôle Bentham thought the legislators would perform in his ideal republic. For in this most unBurkean of governments, Bentham saw the representative in a surprisingly Burkean way. The people would not be the formulators of public policy. The science of legislation would remain a difficult one and the ordinary man would always be far too busy to give adequate consideration to what ought to be done:

> In the exercise of political power, whatsoever is done by the possessors of the supreme power must be done through agents: for as to actual governing, for this, it is admitted, the people are essentially unapt: and on this inaptitude proceeds the proposition, that for the exercise of the operative functions of government, in the highest degree, they should choose agents, who will naturally be some among themselves. On the part of these possessors of the supreme power, moral aptitude can of itself avail little, except in so far as it contributes to the choice of morally apt agents.[36]

The people would be the supreme rulers in that they would select their agents but, after that, 'you will have the goodness to remember that nothing is there for these supreme rulers to do: nothing but to judge of that which has been done by those by whom every thing has been done', i.e. the legislators.[37] Though the people locate and may dislocate their representatives, they are 'not to give direction, either *individual* or *specific*, to their measures, nor therefore to *reward* or *punish* them, except in so far as *relocation* may operate as reward, and *dislocation* as punishment'.[38] These representatives would be, in the main, from the relatively better-off sections of society, a fact necessitated by the low pay and the requirement of unintermittent attendance in the legislature which would make it impossible to earn a living through some other occupation held simultaneously. Moreover, Bentham believed that it was unlikely that the people would choose from their own kind, since familiarity with their equals would not breed sufficient respect to entrust them with such responsibility.[39]

It would not be amiss to suggest that Bentham expected that the legislature would be filled with men like himself, relatively wealthy, educated and independent of mind. These representatives would debate issues on the basis of their own understanding of what would best promote the greatest happiness of the greatest number in the country as a whole. Although elected from districts, they were not to be merely representatives of those districts. Should any given member discover that his understanding of what ought to be done under the greatest happiness principle differed from that of his constituents, it was his duty to act as he thought best and to try to convince them that his stand was the correct one. Should he fail to convince them, they could, of course, remove him at the next annual election. Bentham, however, recognised that there were issues where the feelings of the inhabitants of a district might be so strong that even the most able representative would not be able to convince them that his understanding was correct. As a consequence his services would be lost to the country as a whole. Bentham sought a way out of such an unhappy situation:

> If, on this or that particular occasion, in the opinion of Constituents, or in the opinion of their Deputy, a conflict should have place between their particular aggregate interest and the national interest, he will not be considered as violating his duty to the public, by giving his vote in favour of that same particular interest. For, the national interest being nothing more than an aggregate of the several particular interests, if against that which has been regarded as being the national interest, there be a majority, this result will prove, that in the so declared opinion of that same majority, that, which had been spoken of as if it were the national interest, was not so. If, in support of that which, by a *majority* of his *Constituents*, is regarded as being their interest, there be *not a majority* in the *Legislature*, his vote will be of no effect; and, to the national interest, no evil will have been done by it. On the other hand, a practice, which in every case is evil, is *insincerity:* and in this case, by the supposition on good at all, therefore no preponderant good would be produced by it.
>
> Accordingly, if so it should happen, that, after *speaking* in *support* of an arrangement, which in the opinion of his Constituents, is contrary to their particular interest, he gives his vote *against* that same arrangement, – in such conduct there is not any real inconsistency. By his *speech*, his duty to the *public* is fulfilled; by his *vote*, his duty to his Constituents.[40]

One might well see this as an all too typical piece of Benthamic reasoning, designed as it is to cut the Gordian knot by a relatively simple distinction. Be that as it may, Bentham embraced the distinction because he believed, apparently, that there would be few issues where such conflicts would arise. Certainly he thought that there would be few important occasions where a majority of the representatives, being themselves correct, would be unable to convince their constituents of the incorrectness of their opinions.

Bentham was convinced that the representatives produced by his system could succeed in leading the public to accept policies which would promote not only the greatest happiness of the greatest number but the greatest happiness of all the members of the society so far as was humanly possible. He recognised that his assertion that each man prefers his own self-interest on all occasions applied not merely to rulers but to the public at large. Ultimately self-interest must always prevail, or the human species itself would become extinct. But the ratio between self-interest and social interest ought to be reduced to the smallest one possible. This could only be brought about by the slow and tedious process of the art and science of moral and political cultivation. The legislators would do this by indicating to the people the advantages to be gained by embracing actions conformable to the social interest and by bestowing praise on those individuals who did conform their conduct to the dictates of beneficence and benevolence.[41] It would not be going too far to see such legislators as the elected educators of the people.

But how would one get such legislators, subject as they were to annual election and paid only a minimal salary? Would men of such considerable ability be willing to stand for an office where they would be dependent upon a public which might be quite fickle? Where the failure to convince the inhabitants of one's district of the correctness of one's views would result in being turned out of office? Would not such an office fall inevitably into the hands of second-rate men, all too willing to do whatever the majority in their constituency desired, even when it was detrimental to the majority's own interest? Or to second-rate men who would subserviently approve whatever was recommended to them by the permanent and professional civil service?

Bentham did not think so. As has already been shown on more than one occasion, he consistently held that it was only depraved English lawyers and politicians who believed that the principal, indeed the only, motive which led men to seek political office was the incentive of money, either in itself or in the form of factitious dignity. There were other incentives to office, including the desire for the glory and the honour to be won by serving one's fellow men. Writing in 1830, Bentham denied that he was an 'old and gloomy-minded man' with a very mean picture of human nature, or that he rejected the possibility of such qualities as 'disinterestedness', 'philanthropy' or a 'disposition to self-sacrifice'. On the contrary, he insisted:

> Yes: I admit the existence of *disinterestedness* in the sense in which you mean it. I admit the existence of *philanthropy* – of philanthropy even to an all-comprehensive extent. How could I do otherwise than admit it? My children! I have not far to look for it. Without it, how could so many papers that have preceded this letter, have come into existence? I admit the existence of a disposition to self-sacrifice: How could I do otherwise?[42]

Putting aside the elements of rhetorical exaggeration and self-flattery in such remarks, it is nevertheless true that Bentham did believe that men of talent and moral probity would be attracted to the office of representative, with all of its hazards and handicaps, because they would be motivated by interests such as honour, benevolence and other noble sentiments which he never for a moment denied existed in human nature. Indeed, once the corrupt and corrupting men who held office in countries like England were swept from office, men of active virtue and intelligence who previously disdained political office would willingly consider offering their services to their country. Were the proper form of government established, freed from factitious honour, without the grand superiority of a powerful monarch and the superiority given to opulence merely as opulence, then 'sympathy, and esteem, and thence free and spontaneous service in all its shapes, would attach itself to superiority in the scale of genuine moral virtue: of effective benevolence, in harmony and alliance with self-regarding prudence'.[43]

But in arguing that men of moral probity would be attracted to serve as representatives, Bentham in no way believed that public vigilance should be relaxed. It would be criminal folly to believe that benevolence would keep the representative from abusing his trust. Even the best of men would be corrupted and would seek their own self-interest at the expense of others, unless they were given overpowering reasons for not doing so. If there were exceptions to this rule, men who would remain benevolent regardless of the temptation, they would be so rare that no sensible person would depend upon them. The tendency to misrule was, for all intents and purposes, universal and could only be checked by an extraordinary combination of circumstances. Bentham's *Constitutional Code* was intended to embody such a combination of circumstances. As C. W. Everett has written:

> Bentham's whole code is based, in one sense, on a class struggle, based on a conflict of interest between the only two classes that matter. These classes are not, as the Marxists have supposed, those who own the tools of production and those who do not. Given your democratic state, whence monarchy and aristocratic privilege have disappeared, whence even the special privilege attached to the owning of property has disappeared, Bentham's class struggle has just begun. That is why one must have a Constitutional Code. For the great conflict Bentham saw at the end of his life, as he had seen it at the beginning, was between the governors and the governed. The interests of the governors of a democratic state are *not* those of the governed. To make them so is the task of a Constitutional Code.[44]

The governors, whether legislators or administrators, could take care of themselves – perhaps all too well; and that is why it was necessary to stack the cards on the side of the governed. In the conflict between the sheep and the wolves, it is not the wolves who need protection.

Only when the governors realised that their stay in office would be radically dependent on the governed would they actually serve the greatest happiness of the greatest number. Even with the checks provided by the *Constitutional Code*, there would be the danger of misrule and of corruption although these would be kept to the minimum. It would always be necessary for the wellbeing of society to permit inequalities of wealth, moral virtue and intellectual aptitude to exist, but each of these attributes might be a source of evil, as each was subject to misuse. This was especially true since one form of inequality has a tendency to draw other forms of inequality to itself. Wealth breeds power and factitious honour. Intellectual and moral accomplishments not kept subservient by the greatest vigilance upon the part of the public may lull the people to sleep, to a false sense of security:

> In every political state the whole body of public functionaries constituting the supreme operative require to be considered in the character of corruptors and corruptees: at the best, they are at all times exposed to the temptation of being so, and in a greater or less degree are sure to be made to yield to that temptation. In a republic the sinister effect of that temptation is capable of being confined within bounds – within such bounds as will exclude all practical evil. Under that form of government the constitutive authority is placed over the supreme operative, with dislocative power with relation to it, as well as locative.[45]

The public must keep a careful eye on legislators and administrators alike, lest they corrupt one another to the detriment of the greatest happiness of the greatest number. Only when such suspicion exists will the services that can be rendered to the public be actually given. Only when public officials realise that natural honour depends on the performance of their duty will moral probity on their part be assured. If the legislators are the elected educators of the people, they and the administrators, in their turn, are morally trained by the people, trained via the ballot to desire to do what they ought to do.

In a nation enlightened and made morally sound in this way, Bentham believed that there would be few instances when the interests of the majority would conflict with the interests of the minority, aside from cases involving obviously criminal types. If, after this process of mutual moral education, there were still occasions when even the enlightened interest of the greatest number could only be served by sacrificing the interest of some minority, that was unfortunate. But what would be the alternative? Clearly it would be to sacrifice the interests of the majority to that of the minority, a sacrifice which would be indefensible under the greatest happiness principle. It is doubtful whether John Stuart Mill intended that the genuine interest of the majority ought to be sacrificed to that of any minority. But clearly he felt that Bentham had erred in the assessment of the people he had made in his later years. Mill, like *The Federalist* which Bentham praised in the *Constitutional Code* as 'the work which contains by far the greatest quantity of sound reasoning and useful instruction on the subject of government',[46] had a rather different view of the probity and intelligence of the public. But the difference for Mill and *The Federalist* was not simply over the attributes of individual human beings. Although *The Federalist*, in the tradition of Hobbes, described men as 'ambitious, vindictive, and rapacious',[47] the real problem of representative government was that men, in society, aggregate their interests into factions:

> Among the numerous advantages promised by a well-constructed Union, none deserves to be more accurately developed than its tendency to break and control the violence of faction. The friend of popular governments never finds himself so much alarmed for their character and fate, as when he contemplates their propensity to this dangerous vice. He will not fail, therefore, to set a due value on any plan which, without violating the principles to which he is attached, provides a proper cure for it. The instability, injustice, and confusion introduced into the public councils, have, in truth, been the mortal diseases under which popular governments have everywhere perished; as they continue to be the favorite and fruitful topics from which the adversaries to liberty derive their most specious declamations. . . . Complaints are everywhere heard from our most considerate and virtuous citizens, equally the friends of public and private faith, and of public and personal liberty, that our governments are too unstable, that the public good is disregarded in the conflicts of rival parties, and that measures are too often decided, not according to the rules of justice and the rights of the minor party, but by the superior force of an interested and overbearing majority.[48]

The purpose behind the structure of the United States Constitution, including the separation of powers, checks and balances, and the federal system itself, was to prevent injustice and to control the evils of faction, whether caused by a minority or the majority.

These devices, however, were not intended to prevent justifiable majority rule but to check the possibility of majority tyranny. But

Bentham scorned the necessity of balance as much as he scorned the notion that justice was the end of government. Concerning *The Federalist*, he wrote:

> But justice, what is it that we are to understand by justice: and why not happiness but justice? What happiness is, every man knows, because, what pleasure is, every man knows, and what pain is, every man knows. But what justice is, – this is what on every occasion is the subject-matter of dispute. Be the meaning of the word justice what it will, what regard is it entitled to otherwise than as a means of happiness[?][49]

Bentham did recognise that there were aggregated interests or factions, but he apparently saw them only among minorities.

> The danger which the probity of a public man is exposed to, from the suggestions of his own immediate interest, is trifling in comparison with the attacks it has to sustain from the interests of all sorts which surround him. Amongst these, local and professional interests are particularly dangerous. Individual ones venture not beyond a whisper: the others, by their clamour counterfeit the public voice, and clothe themselves impudently in the garb of virtue.[50]

But the great majority was a collectivity without any such common interest. It was not they but groups such as lawyers and churchmen who threaten the probity of public men. It is possible, even likely, that the praise Bentham bestowed on the majority was exaggerated in the hope of putting to rest unwarranted concerns about the majority. Moreover, Bentham could in fairness ask whether any harm the majority might do to any minority could possibly exceed the harm that was being done to the majority by the ruling minorities under the existing regime. But the plan proposed in the *Constitutional Code* seems to depend on Bentham's belief that the majority was made up of discrete individuals who shared but one common interest so far as government was concerned and that was the desire not to be harmed. Like sheep in a flock they only wanted protection:

> In a representative democracy, take any one member of the community acting in the exercise of the supreme constitutive power. His desire is to afford to himself security against depredation and oppression: such being his ultimate desire, his intermediate desire is – to see located in the situation of his representative, a man who, desire and power in all shapes included, appears to him likely to contribute, in a degree more than any other man would, to his possession of that same security: such is his desire, and such

> accordingly is his act, – the act by which he gives his vote. For the gratification of any sinister desire at the expense of the universal interest, he cannot hope to find co-operation and support from any considerable number of his fellow citizens.[51]

Bentham may have been led to this belief by what he saw as the far too great willingness of the people to tolerate the abuses of the English Government and their failure to act in concert to put a stop to such abuses. It may also have been due to the fact that he thought the vast majority of men would always have to spend the better part of their time working to earn enough to survive so that there would be no time left for them to think about banding together in what today would be called interest groups or labour unions. In any case, it is ironic that Bentham, the friend and intellectual father of Sir Francis Place, should have built so many hopes on an assumption that was being called into question by Place's activity. For in the very years that Bentham was writing the *Constitutional Code*, Place was working to raise the status and organise the 'political action' of the working class. He was 'the first to develop the modern arts of lobbying' and to teach the workers how to bring pressure to bear on Parliament.[52] It remained, then, for Mill to wonder whether the success of Place and others who followed him rendered the entire scheme proposed in the *Constitutional Code* open to question.

Notes Chapter V

1 *Works*, IX, p. 5 (*Constitutional Code*).
2 ibid., pp. 62–3, 114–17. See also Bentham, 'Anti-Senatica', ed. and with an Introduction by Charles Warren Everett, *Smith College Studies in History*, vol. XI (July, 1926), pp. 209–67.
3 *Works*, IX, pp. 98–113, 155–7.
4 ibid., p. 160. See also ibid., pp. 119–24.
5 ibid.
6 ibid., p. 207.
7 ibid., p. 204.
8 ibid., p. 206.
9 ibid., pp. 205, 266–94.
10 For what follows, see ibid., pp. 59–63. More detailed summaries of the structure of government proposed in the *Constitutional Code* may be found in Thomas P. Peardon, 'Bentham's Ideal Republic', *Canadian Journal of Economics & Political Science*, vol. XVII (May 1951), pp. 184–203, and Charles Warren Everett, 'The Constitutional Code of Jeremy Bentham', *Jeremy Bentham Bicentenary Celebrations* (London, H. K. Lewis, 1948), pp. 1–29.
11 J. S. Mill, 'Bentham', *Essays on Ethics, Religion and Society*, in the *Collected Works of John Stuart Mill*, vol. X (Toronto, University of Toronto Press, 1969), p. 106.

12 ibid.
13 ibid., pp. 106–7.
14 ibid., p. 107.
15 *Works*, I, p. 231 (*A Fragment on Government*).
16 *Works*, II, p. 522 (*Anarchical Fallacies*).
17 UC 44, p. 2; *Works*, II, p. 522 (*Anarchical Fallacies*).
18 UC 44, pp. 2, 4, 5; *Economic Writings*, I, pp. 130–1, 156–61 (*Defence of Usury*).
19 *Works*, IX, p. 62.
20 ibid., p. 97.
21 ibid., p. 98.
22 On bills of rights see *IPML*, pp. 308–11; *Works*, II, pp. 500–3 (*Anarchical Fallacies*); on judge-made law see *OLG*, pp. 239–41; on opposition to the notion of 'balance' in a constitution and, hence, on behalf of a unicameral legislature, see *Works*, I, pp. 277–83 (*A Fragment on Government*); UC 146, pp. 19–23. Consider, also, Bentham's defence of the House of Lords in *Economic Writings*, I, pp. 328–32 (*Supply without Burthen*). Finally, J. H. Burns, 'Bentham on Sovereignty: An Exploration', *Bentham and Legal Theory*, ed. M. H. James, *Northern Ireland Legal Quarterly*, vol. XXIV (1973), provides an important discussion of the development of Bentham's thought.
23 *Works*, IX, pp. 59, 112.
24 ibid., pp. 45–6.
25 ibid., pp. 104–5.
26 ibid., p. 53.
27 See *Works*, IX, pp. 2, 26, 145; UC 111, pp. 40, 53–4, 166–8; Additional Manuscripts of the British Museum, 33,551, pp. 14, 32. But for some rather harsh strictures on the evils of the English system, see *Works*, IX, pp. 9–10, 59–60, 73, 127.
28 UC 97, p. 37.
29 *Works*, I, pp. 358–64 (*Of the Levelling System*); *Works*, II, pp. 496–7, 525–6, 533–4 (*Anarchical Fallacies*).
30 UC 125, p. 340.
31 *Works*, IX, p. 76.
32 ibid. In general, see also ibid., pp. 64–95 and UC 111, pp. 122–4, 152–61, 268–9, 271, 275.
33 *Works*, IX, pp. 143–4 and UC 125, pp. 357–8.
34 *Works*, IX, p. 43.
35 ibid., pp. 37–9, 41–6, 54–8, 166, 232–53, 260–4; UC 125, pp. 363–6, 368; UC 126, pp. 145–7, 392–3.
36 *Works*, IX, p. 98.
37 UC 125, p. 360.
38 *Works*, IX, p. 153.
39 ibid., p. 117; UC 127, p. 439.
40 *Works*, IX, pp. 160–1.
41 UC 125, pp. 203–5. The process of identifying the self-regarding and the social interest is treated, *in extentio*, in UC 14, pp. 197–214 and UC 15, pp. 3–125. These manuscripts were intended to be published in a work entitled 'Deontology'. Although Bowring did publish a work with that title under Bentham's name, it is generally agreed that there is little resemblance between it and the manuscripts.
42 *Works*, IV, p. 431 (*On Houses of Peers and Senates*).

43 *Works*, IX, p. 81. Also UC 111, pp. 61–5.
44 C. W. Everett, 'The Constitutional Code of Jeremy Bentham', op. cit., p. 289. See *Works*, IX, pp. 49, 101–3, 153; UC 111, pp. 108–9, 210–14; UC 125, pp. 14, 378–81.
45 *Works*, IX, p. 69. Also ibid., pp. 49, 80–3, 101–3.
46 ibid., p. 123. Also UC 125, p. 342.
47 Alexander Hamilton, John Jay and James Madison, *The Federalist*, no. 6 (New York, Modern Library, 1937), p. 27.
48 *The Federalist*, no. 10, pp. 53–4.
49 *Works*, IX, p. 123.
50 ibid., p. 125.
51 ibid., p. 100. Also UC 125, pp. 207, 305–6; UC 126, p. 240.
52 G. M. Trevelyan, *British History in the Nineteenth Century and After: 1782–1919*, pp. 201–2.

Conclusion

From the beginning until the end of his life Bentham was above all other things a reformer. Even his more erudite speculations, such as those on language and mathematics, were typically intended to contribute to change in the moral and political life of society. But unlike many reformers, Bentham sought to be comprehensive in his suggestions and to ground his proposals firmly on a science of morals and legislation. That science, in its turn, was to be based on observation, experience and, where possible, experimentation. If the fundamental goal for the science, the pursuit of the greatest happiness of the greatest number, was fixed, nevertheless the science itself was intended to be flexible, ever ready to take into account new information and new suggestions as to how the end might best be achieved. Thus when Bentham became a democrat it was because he believed the evidence indicated that democracy was necessary and possible: evidence from the United States indicated that a democracy could be stable and therefore democracy was a viable form of government; evidence from England indicated that change there was necessary because corruption and the abuse of liberty were inherent in the institutional arrangements of government. But, having become a democrat, Bentham's concern for flexibility and for empirical evidence seems to have abandoned him. Perhaps this was the result of the long and bitter frustrations which he had experienced over the years in his attempts to win support for reform. But perhaps it also reveals something about the nature of his enterprise from the beginning.

One can exaggerate Bentham's inflexibility in his later years. It seems likely that the excess in his attack on the English Government was designed, in part, to frighten the governors and to stir the governed so that at least partial reformation might be won fairly quickly and the worst evils thereby alleviated though not fully cured. Partial change would not result in the best of all possible worlds but it would be better than the degeneracy which he felt was then afflicting England. Bentham was still a gradualist. And, after all, the government of the United States was also remote in many respects from Bentham's ideal republic but this did not prevent him from praising the United States, however critical he was of the ways in which it fell short of his ideal. Nor did Bentham believe that everything he was proposing was final and sacrosanct. He recognised that future experience might prove that alterations were necessary, and he condemned constitutions which attempted to prevent future change through a bill of rights or a complicated system of checks and balances. The very structure of the government he proposed made change, including fundamental change, in principle, easy to accomplish.[1]

Granting these remnants of flexibility and granting also that his view of human nature was more complex than his critics admit, the fact remains that the government proposed in the *Constitutional Code* was not based on actual political experience but was derived from the notion that the guiding question for political thought was how to prevent misrule, given the prevalence of self-interest on the part of every individual. It is true that Bentham believed that he had demonstrated, on the basis of experience, that self-interest was, and, indeed, had to be the prevalent characteristic of human nature. But by concentrating on that factor and that factor alone in the decisive respect, Bentham was led to propose a form of government whose keystone was the necessity of suspicion and distrust upon the part of the governed in their attitude toward the governors. Only by constantly distrusting the governors could the governed protect themselves against misrule. But one is compelled to wonder what a society would be like which depended for its wellbeing on such suspicion and distrust. Bentham himself had written in the *Rationale of Judicial Evidence*, which it should be noted was edited for him by John Stuart Mill, that:

> The disposition or propensity to belief may, . . ., be said to be stronger than the disposition, the propensity, to disbelief. Were the proposition reversed, the business of society could not be carried on – society itself could not have had existence; for the facts which fall under the perception of any given individual are in number but as a drop of water in the bucket, compared with those concerning the existence of which it is impossible for him to obtain any persuasion otherwise than from the reports, the assertions, made by other men.[2]

One can only speculate, albeit guided by relevant experience when possible, on what might happen were the suspicion and distrust which Bentham called for to actually come into existence. Would not such a spirit result in alienation and estrangement from government or, perhaps, to widespread disobedience? Would not the people, in suspecting every move the government made, develop a disposition toward suspicion and distrust in their fellow men in general and not just toward the governors? Or, given the fact that men do associate in groups, would not the result be the hostile struggle of those groups to extract from the government whatever was thought to be in the interest of the group without any concern for the interests of others or the damage done to the public as a whole? Or, given the fact of political parties (which would in no way be prevented in Bentham's ideal republic), would not the consequence be that positions within the administration would be distributed under a spoils system similar to that which developed in the United States as a result of Jacksonian democracy?[3]

It is unlikely that Bentham would have been happy with any of these possibilities. Throughout his career he stressed the need for what is usually called deference but what he called obsequiousness. As late as 1821, he wrote:

> Everywhere, and at all times, on the part of the subject-many, howsoever treated, exists the disposition to obsequiousness. *Birth*, observation of the direction taken by *rewards* and *punishments*, by *praise* and *dispraise*, of the habit and language of all around; – by the concurrence of all these causes the disposition is produced, and kept up.
>
> To alter or weaken this disposition, in such sort as to produce revolution in government, or considerable mischief to person or property of individuals, nothing ever has sufficed, or ever can suffice, short of the extremity of misrule.[4]

Yet precisely in that government where misrule was said to be least likely, suspicion and distrust were apparently to replace obsequiousness. In fact, Bentham did not want nor did he expect the end to obsequiousness as such but only to that form of it which takes place through the influence of one person's will upon that of another. Deference should not be paid to the titled or the wealthy. Deference should exist where there is the influence of the understanding upon the understanding, i.e. the people ought to defer to men who have knowledge and, in particular, knowledge of the art and science of morals and legislation.[5]

Appropriate obsequiousness (to use Bentham's harsh but revealing terminology) is connected, then, with the nature of the art and science of morals and legislation. But, in fact, there are some profound difficulties within that art and science – difficulties of such a nature that an adequate analysis would carry us far beyond the scope of this study precisely because it would carry us far beyond the limits of Bentham's thought. For what he said in these respects is either incomplete or confused or both. Only a few indications of the difficulties which exist within his system can be made here. Bentham consistently maintained that the end to be pursued was the greatest happiness of the greatest number, hedonically measured. The touchstone for understanding what happiness was, was to understand the feelings of the people. As has been shown, Bentham maintained that what an individual's feelings are is evident to the individual as individual. No man knows what justice is but every man knows what brings him pleasure or causes him pain. One may well wonder whether this is true, save perhaps in the case of the simplest of pleasures and pains. Certainly Bentham himself did not act as if he believed it was true. The science of morals and legislation is the most difficult of enterprises. Only a few can see the connection between given actions and consequent pleasures or pains. Only a few can understand the springs of human actions and how to employ the various sanctions in order to promote pleasure and prevent pain. Few can master the difficult system of classification which the science demands, and few are able to penetrate beyond the fictions and fallacies of ordinary discourse and understand the truth about real entities. The art and science of morals and legislation is dedicated to the task of enlightening the people to what, in fact, ought or ought not to bring them pleasure and what ought or ought not to cause them pain; and this work of enlightenment is essentially the work of the few and not of the people themselves. The science is a science for legislators who employ it either because they understand it themselves or because they are advised by those who do. And this would be true even in the democracy proposed in the *Constitutional Code*.

Bentham himself had a humane regard for the existing feelings of the people, and he believed that any legislator ought to have a like regard. But, at the same time, he believed that the feelings of the people had to be altered. Certainly some of those alterations were necessary simply because existing feelings caused unnecessary pain to others. But that was not the sole reason for change. Thus to teach the people to be tolerant in matters of religion would end the pain caused through persecution or social hostility. But Bentham did not intend to let it go at that. He hoped that religion would, sooner or later, be extirpated because he believed that religion prevented the individual as individual from seeking his own greatest happiness and made him an all too likely victim of deceptive reasoning.[6] But to argue in such a manner apparently presumes knowledge of what happiness is, entirely aside from the feelings of the people. Or, to take another example, suppose that the people did not feel that the government proposed in the *Constitutional Code* was, for them, the best form of government; that they felt that their happiness could best be achieved under some form of government quite different from Bentham's ideal republic; that they proved as resistant to his suggestions for change as had the English rulers?

Would Bentham have simply deferred to the correctness of their feelings? The fact is that he did not do so, but rather described them as foolish and deluded in their attachment to the existing regime which caused them pain whether they knew it or not. In short, Bentham distrusted the feelings of the people on many important subjects.

This distrust did not lead Bentham to propose that a revolutionary party seize control and establish his best regime without regard to the feelings of the people. The feelings of the people would have to be changed by persuasion and not by force. The people would have to be led to accept the constitution proposed in the *Code*. Bentham recognised that it might take time to win acceptance, perhaps a hundred years or more. For a reformer, his patience was extraordinary. But that patience ought not to obscure the fact that, were his ideal republic established, legislation would be the work of experts and not of the people. Popular acceptance of both legislation and the *Code* would have to be obtained. But the way in which Bentham thought that approval would be won suggests some interesting difficulties in his theory of the influence of the understanding on the understanding.

These difficulties are exemplified by Bentham's *Auto-Icon; or Further Uses of the Dead to the Living* which he wrote sometime during the last decade or so of his life. In that little pamphlet he described how mummified bodies of both benefactors and malefactors might be displayed in order to provide graphic examples of the benefits to be gained or the penalties to be paid for rendering society more happy or causing it to be less happy. But for Bentham, who had himself mummified and who is now on display at University College, London, this suggestion was no late aberration nor the product of a diseased and senile mind. He had made similar suggestions early in his life.[7] It was connected with a belief which he held throughout his life that the great majority of people are not simply moved by reason. The influence of the understanding on the understanding could take place in two ways: an appeal might be made directly to the reasoning faculty; or it might be made to the passions and the imagination. Bentham occasionally held that the people were blind only for want of a little age and the want of experience which would quickly be remedied once they were given the vote. But his more frequent argument was that on most occasions, appeals about the beneficent or malificent character of actions would have to be made to the passions and the imagination:

> Preach to the eye, if you would preach with efficacy. By that organ, through the medium of the imagination, the judgment of the bulk of mankind may be led and moulded almost at pleasure. As puppets in the hand of the showman, so would men be in the hand of the

legislator, who, to the science proper to his function, should add a well-informed attention to stage effect.[8]

Perhaps even more revealing is Bentham's discussion of how the Panopticon architectural scheme might be used for purposes of education. He recognised the concern some might have over the 'constant and unremitting pressure' the system would give to the educator. Although he may have overestimated the 'herculean and ineludible strength' which it would place in the hands of the schoolmaster, nevertheless his reply to such concerns is of interest:

> Would *happiness* be most likely to be increased or diminished by this discipline? – Call them soldiers, call them monks, call them machines: so they were but happy ones, I should not care. Wars and storms are best to read of, but peace and calms are better to enjoy. Don't be frightened now, my dear *****, and think that I am going to entertain you with a course of moral philosophy, or even with a system of education. Happiness is a very pretty thing to feel, but very dry to talk about; so you may unknit your brow, for I shall say no more about the matter. One thing only I will add, which is, that whoever sets up an inspection-school upon the tiptop of the principle, had need to be very sure of the master; for the boy's body is not more the child of his father's, than his mind will be of the master's mind; with no other difference than what there is between *command* on the one side and *subjection* on the other.[9]

Although Bentham tried to dismiss the discussion of education in the *Panopticon* as 'a sort of *jeu d'esprit*, which would hardly have presented itself in so light a form, at any other period than at the moment of conception, and under the flow of spirits which the charms of novelty are apt enough to inspire',[10] in fact it indicates a persistent problem in his thought. The legislators, particularly when equipped with the Benthamic science of morals and legislation, would be the educators of the public. What would prevent them from manipulating the public as a showman manipulates his puppets? What if such power should fall, as it had in the past, into the hands of those like the churchmen who praised as saints men who, in Bentham's eyes, had caused divisiveness and unhappiness? Or who condemned as sinners and atheists men like Locke who had been the benefactors of mankind?

Such problems were not lost on Bentham. He knew that knowledge, as much as riches and factitious dignity, was a form of power, and that, without moral probity, the greater that power the greater the chance for misrule. He also knew that deceptive reasoning could not legally be banished and that, therefore, there would always be the danger that men of reason might use their power to lead the people to do that which was not in their own best interest.[11] That is why the people must be so suspicious and distrustful of those who would be their masters, and why they must be given the fullest power of choosing and dislocating those masters. The suspicion and distrust of the people was to fall, in the first and fullest instance, on the members of the legislative body. Bentham was concerned that this might weaken the independence of mind of the legislators themselves, but he saw no other way of ensuring their probity and dedication to the public good.[12] But if they were weakened in this way could they perform the task of enlightenment which was necessary to lead the people to achieve their own greatest happiness? Might not the legislators, as at times Bentham feared, in their anxiety to stay in office defer to the wishes of their constituents even though they knew that, in doing so, they were endangering the long-range interest of the public? Although Bentham argued that such behaviour was analogous to a legislator in a mixed monarchy selling his independence in return for a gift,[13] it is not at all clear how his ideal republic would prevent this from happening unless one presumes that a majority of the voters in a majority of the constituencies were already enlightened in such a manner that they would listen to the direct appeal of reason. But Bentham seems to have discounted that as a possibility not only for his own time but for the future. And if the legislators were not controlled by suspicion and distrust, if they were independent minded, what would prevent them from manipulating the public, turning the people into soldiers or monks or robots, albeit happy ones?

Ultimately such problems are rooted in Bentham's nominalism. We have suggested that the end of the science of morals and legislation was fixed. But, in fact, happiness is an abstract word. What happiness is varies in important respects from time to time and from place to place. What people consider to be the elements which constitute their happiness depends not on some bedrock physiological or psychological foundation but upon opinion:

> That discourse of all kinds, more especially discourse declarative of opinion, is completely in the power of the will, is manifest enough. But he who is completely master of men's discourses, is little less than completely master of men's opinions. It is by the discourse of A, that the opinion of B is governed, much more than by any reflections of his own. To take upon trust from others (that is, from the discourses of others) his own opinions, is, on by far the greater part of the subjects that come under his cognizance and call upon him in

> one way or other for his decision, the lot, the inevitable lot, of the wisest and most cautious among mankind: how much more frequently so, that of the ignorant, the rash, the headstrong, the unthinking multitude![14]

Bentham believed, whether one liked it or not, that the people at large were not then, nor would they ever be, the masters of opinion. How could the people understand what happiness was in complicated social and political matters when they erred even in respect to sexual pleasure, believing, because they followed the wrong masters, that such things as homosexuality ought to be condemned?[15] If public opinion was improving, it was because the public was beginning to listen to men like Bentham instead of churchmen, lawyers, aristocrats, kings and poets. Bentham believed, as much as Mill, that progress was the work of the few, not the many. But he also believed that the few when corrupted, as they were in England, were much greater threats to progress than were the many. In Mill's eyes, however, the spirit of distrust and suspicion fostered by Bentham's arguments had already made the people unwilling to defer to those whose knowledge was superior – those who knew and understood the superior pleasure of a dissatisfied Socrates to a satisfied fool or pig.[16] Thus, for Mill, the dominance of the unthinking multitude, who did not and could not have an adequate vision of mankind's highest aspirations, threatened the possibility of progress toward genuine happiness. But to know what genuinely constitutes progress, one would seem to have to have some standard by which to measure improvement, a standard which was right entirely aside from the changing opinions of the people and their masters. Neither Bentham nor Mill was able to provide an adequate account of what it means to speak of progress within an utilitarian ethic: why a free, energetic but discontented public is superior (or inferior) to complacent but happy automatons. Or why, idiosyncrasy aside, it is better to be a frustrated reformer like Bentham than to be a contented placeman or sinecurist.

Bentham's failure, in the last analysis, to resolve such problems ought not to be taken simply as a criticism of him. Others who came after him lacked his tenacity in confronting such difficulties as those posed by the relationship of opinion to truth, democratic society to science and ordinary people to experts. A considerable number of thinkers have since decided that it is impossible to have a cognitive ethic, and, as a consequence, the attempt to establish a rational science of morals and legislation has been replaced by value-free social science which rejects the notion of objectively valid evaluations about the worth of various forms of happiness. But one must wonder whether the freedom from choice of value-free social science has not been purchased at the price of sterility. One may well prefer to begin to re-examine the nature and purpose of political thought by confronting the problems left unresolved by Bentham's endeavours, rather than accept the all too easy solutions of many who came after him.

Notes Conclusion

1 *Works*, IX, pp. 3, 119–24. See also Warren Roberts, 'Bentham's Conception of Political Change: A Liberal Approach', *Political Studies*, IX (October 1961), pp. 254–66.
2 *Works*, VI, p. 236 (*Rationale of Judicial Evidence*).
3 See, for example, *Identity and Anxiety*, eds Maurice Stein, Arthur J. Vidich and David Manning White (Glencoe, Ill., The Free Press, 1960); Robert Paul Wolff, *The Poverty of Liberalism* (Boston, Mass., The Beacon Press, 1968); and Leonard D. White, *The Jacksonians* (New York, Macmillan, 1956).
4 *Works*, II, p. 287 (*On Liberty of Public Discussion*).
5 UC 125, pp. 16–17, 37–8, 40, 48–50; UC 126, pp. 107–11, 120–32.
6 *Works*, IX, pp. 92–5. See also my 'Morality and Belief: The Origin and Purpose of Bentham's Writings on Religion', *The Mill News Letter*, VI (Spring 1971), pp. 3–15.
7 One of the few printed (but unpublished) copies of the *Auto-Icon* may be found in The British Library. One extant manuscript page may be found in UC 149, p. 204. For early related suggestions see, for example, UC 70, p. 117; UC 87, p. 66; UC 98, p. 170.
8 *Works*, VI, p. 321. Cf. UC 126, p. 393 with p. 180 and *Works*, VI, pp. 318–21; *Works*, VII, pp. 76–115, 280–3, 287, 297, 455–7 (*Rationale of Judicial Evidence*).
9 *Works*, IV, pp. 63–4 (*Panopticon, . . .*).
10 ibid., p. 40.
11 *Works*, IX, pp. 81, 110–12, 116; UC 126, pp. 127–8, 131, 181–5.
12 UC 126, pp. 229, 243–5.
13 UC 126, pp. 244–5.
14 *Works*, VII, p. 108 (*Rationale of Judicial Evidence*). See also UC 125, pp. 24–5. For what follows see J. J. C. Smart, *An Outline of a System of Utilitarian Ethics* (Melbourne, Melbourne University Press, 1961), and Leo Strauss, *Natural Right and History* (Chicago, The University of Chicago Press, 1953), especially pp. 1–80.
15 See, in particular, UC 74, pp. 35–222 and UC 161, pp. 1–523, manuscripts which Bentham intended for *Not Paul, But Jesus*, part of which was edited for him by Francis Place and published under the pseudonym of Gamaliel Smith (London, John Hunt, 1823).
16 J. S. Mill, 'Utilitarianism', *Essays on Ethics, Religion and Society*, in the *Collected Works of John Stuart Mill*, vol. X (Toronto, University of Toronto Press, 1969), pp. 210–12.

Bibliography

A BENTHAM'S WORKS

Manuscripts

Additional Manuscripts of the British Museum (London)

University College Bentham Manuscript Collection, University College Library (London)

Others

Analysis of the Influence of Natural Religion on the Temporal Happiness of Mankind, by 'Philip Beauchamp' (London, R. Carlile, 1822)

Anti-Senatica, ed. and with an Introduction by C. W. Everett, *Smith College Studies in History*, XI (July 1926), pp. 209–67

Auto-Icon, or Further Uses of the Dead to the Living. A Fragment (London, 1842 [?])

Bentham's Theory of Fictions, with an Introduction by C. K. Ogden (London, Kegan Paul, Trench, Trubner, 1932)

Church-of-Englandism and its Catechism examined (London, Effingham Wilson, 1818)

A Comment on the Commentaries, ed. C. W. Everett (Oxford, Clarendon Press, 1928)

The Correspondence of Jeremy Bentham: 1752–80, ed. T. L. S. Sprigge, 2 vols, *The Collected Works of Jeremy Bentham* (London, Athlone Press, 1968)

The Correspondence of Jeremy Bentham: January 1781–October 1788, ed. Ian R. Christie, *The Collected Works of Jeremy Bentham* (London, Athlone Press, 1971)

An Introduction to the Principles of Morals and Legislation, ed. J. H. Burns and H. L. A. Hart, *The Collected Works of Jeremy Bentham* (London, Athlone Press, 1970)

Jeremy Bentham's Economic Writings, ed. with Introductions by W. Stark, 3 vols (London, George Allen & Unwin, 1952–4)

Not Paul, But Jesus, by 'Gamaliel Smith' (London, John Hunt, 1823)

Of Laws in General, ed. H. L. A. Hart, *The Collected Works of Jeremy Bentham* (London, Athlone Press, 1970)

Theory of Legislation, trans. from the French of Etienne Dumont by Richard Hildreth (London, Trubner, 1876)

The Works of Jeremy Bentham, ed. John Bowring, 11 vols (Edinburgh, William Tait, 1838–43)

B OTHER WORKS

Aristotle, *Nichomachean Ethics*

Aspinall, Arthur, *Politics and the Press c. 1750–1850* (London, Home & Van Thal, 1949)

Baumgardt, David, *Bentham and the Ethics of Today* (New York, Octagon Books, 1966)

Blackstone, Sir William, *Commentaries on the Laws of England*, 15th edn, 4 vols (London, 1809)

Blount, Charles, 'Bentham, Dumont and Mirabeau', *University of Birmingham Historical Journal*, III (1952), pp. 153–67.

BIBLIOGRAPHY

Brebner, J. Bartlet, 'Laissez Faire and State Intervention in Nineteenth-Century Britain', *The Journal of Economic History: Supplement*, VIII (1948), pp. 59–73

Brogan, Sir Denis, 'The Intellectual in Great Britain', *The Intellectual in Politics*, ed. H. Malcolm Macdonald (Austin, The Humanities Research Center of the University of Texas, 1966)

Burkholder, L., 'Tarlton on Bentham's *Fragment on Government*', *Political Studies*, XXI (December 1973), pp. 523–6

Burns, J. H., 'Bentham and the French Revolution', *The Transactions of The Royal Historical Society*, 5th series, XVI (1966), pp. 95–114

Burns, J. H., 'Bentham on Sovereignty: An Exploration', *Bentham and Legal Theory*, ed. M. H. James, *Northern Ireland Legal Quarterly*, XXIV (1973), pp. 133–50

Burns, J. H., *The Fabric of Felicity: the Legislator and the Human Condition*, an Inaugural Lecture delivered at University College London (London, published for the College by H. K. Lewis, 1967)

Cartwright, Major John, *American Independence: The Interest and Glory of Great Britain* (London, 1774; expanded edn, 1775)

Cartwright, Major John, *Take Your Choice!* (London, 1776)

Dicey, A. V. *Lectures on the Relation between Law and Public Opinion during the Nineteenth Century*, 2nd edn (London, Macmillan, 1924)

Everett, C. W. 'The Constitutional Code of Jeremy Bentham', *Jeremy Bentham Bicentenary Celebrations* (London, H. K. Lewis, 1948)

Everett, C. W., *The Education of Jeremy Bentham* (New York, Columbia University Press, 1931)

Finlayson, Geoffrey, *Decade of Reform: England in the Eighteen Thirties* (New York, W. W. Norton, 1970)

Halévy, Elie, *The Growth of Philosophic Radicalism*, trans. Mary Morris (Boston, Mass., The Beacon Press, 1955)

Hamilton, Alexander, Jay, John, and Madison, James, *The Federalist* (New York, Modern Library, 1937)

Hartley, David, *Observations on Man, His Frame, His Duty, and His Expectations* (London, 1749)

Helvetius, C. A., *De L'Esprit or Essays on the Mind and Its Several Faculties*, trans. from the French, 1810 (New York, Burt Franklin, 1970)

Helvetius, C. A., *A Treatise on Man; His Intellectual Faculties and His Education*, trans. from the French with additional notes by W. Hooper, 1810, 2 vols (New York, Burt Franklin, 1970)

Himmelfarb, Gertrude, 'The Haunted House of Jeremy Bentham', *Victorian Minds* (New York, Harper Torchbooks, 1970)

Himmelfarb, Gertrude, 'On Reading Bentham Seriously', *Studies in Burke and his Times*, XIV (Winter 1972–73), pp. 179–86

Hobbes, Thomas, *Leviathan*, ed. and with an Introduction by Michael Oakeshott (Oxford, Basil Blackwell, 1947)

Howley, William (Lord Bishop of London), *A Charge Delivered to the Clergy of the Diocese of London* (London, T. Bensley, 1814)

Hume, David, *A Treatise of Human Nature*, ed. L. A. Selby-Bigge (Oxford, Clarendon Press, 1888)

[Jeffreys, Francis], *The Edinburgh Review*, IV (1804), pp. 1–26

Kant, Immanuel, *Foundations of the Metaphysics of Morals*, trans. Lewis White Beck (Indianapolis, Ind., Bobbs-Merrill, 1959)

Keeton, George W., and Schwarzenberger, Georg, eds, *Jeremy Bentham and the Law: A Symposium* (Westport, Conn., Greenwood Press, 1970)

Letwin, Shirley R., *The Pursuit of Certainty* (Cambridge, University Press, 1965)
Locke, John, *Two Treatises of Government*, ed. and with an Introduction and notes by Peter Laslett (Cambridge, University Press, 1960)
Lyons, David, *In the Interest of the Governed* (Oxford, Clarendon Press, 1973)
Mack, Mary, *Jeremy Bentham: An Odyssey of Ideas 1748–1792* (London, Heinemann, 1962)
Manning, D. H., *The Mind of Jeremy Bentham* (London, Longmans, Green, 1968)
Mill, John Stuart, 'Bentham' and 'Utilitarianism', *Essays on Ethics, Religion and Society*, vol. x, *Collected Works of John Stuart Mill* (Toronto, University of Toronto Press, 1969)
Namier, Sir Lewis, *The Structure of Politics at the Accession of George III*, 2nd edn (London, Macmillan, 1960)
Nietzsche, Friedrich, *Beyond Good and Evil*, trans. and with commentary by Walter Kaufmann (New York, Vintage Books, 1966)
Norris, John, *Shelburne and Reform* (London, Macmillan, 1963)
Oakeshott, Michael, *Rationalism in Politics and Other Essays* (London, Methuen, 1962)
Parekh, Bhikhu, ed., *Jeremy Bentham: Ten Critical Essays* (London, Frank Cass, 1974)
Peardon, Thomas P., 'Bentham's Ideal Republic', *Canadian Journal of Economics & Political Science*, XVII (May, 1951), pp. 184–203
Plamenatz, John, *The English Utilitarians*, revised edn (Oxford, Basil Blackwell, 1958)
Plumb, J. H., *England in the Eighteenth Century* (Baltimore, Md., Penguin Books, 1950)
Pope, Alexander, 'An Essay on Man', *Pope's Poetical Works*, ed. Herbert Davis (London, Oxford University Press, 1966)
Price, Richard, *Observations on the Nature of Civil Liberty, the principles of Government, and the justice and policy of the war with America* (London, 1776)
Radzinowicz, Leon, *A History of English Criminal Law and its Administration from 1750*, 3 vols (New York, Macmillan, 1948, 1957)
Robbins, Lionel, *The Theory of Economic Policy in English Classical Political Economy* (London, Macmillan, 1961)
Roberts, David, *Victorian Origins of the British Welfare State* (New Haven, Conn., Yale University Press, 1960)
Roberts, Warren, 'Bentham's Conception of Political Change: A Liberal Approach', *Political Studies*, IX (October 1961), pp. 254–66
Romilly, Sir Samuel, *The Life of Sir Samuel Romilly, with a selection from His Correspondence*, ed. his sons, 3rd edn, 2 vols (London, John Murray, 1842)
Shelley, Percy, *Poetical Works*, ed. Thomas Hutchinson, a new edition corrected by G. M. Matthews (London, Oxford University Press, 1970)
Sidgwick, Henry, *The Method of Ethics*, 7th edn (New York, Dover Publications, 1966)
Smart, J. J. C., *An Outline of a System of Utilitarian Ethics* (Melbourne, Melbourne University Press, 1961)
Smith, Adam, *The Wealth of Nations* (New York, Modern Library, 1937)
Stein, Maurice, Viditch, Arthur J., and White, David Manning, *Identity and Anxiety* (Glencoe, Ill., The Free Press, 1960)
Steintrager, James, 'Morality and Belief: The Origin and Purpose of Bentham's Writings on Religion', *The Mill News Letter*, VI (Spring 1971), pp. 3–15

Stephen, Leslie, *The English Utilitarians*, 3 vols (London, Duckworth, 1900)
Strauss, Leo, *Natural Right and History* (Chicago, University of Chicago Press, 1953)
Tarlton, Charles D., 'The Overlooked Strategy of Bentham's *Fragment on Government*', *Political Studies*, XX (December 1972), pp. 397–406
Trevelyan, G. M., *British History in the Nineteenth Century and After: 1782–1919* (New York, Harper Torchbooks, 1966)
Twining, W. L. and Twining, P. E., 'Bentham on Torture', *Bentham and Legal Theory*, ed. by M. H. James, *Northern Ireland Legal Quarterly*, XXIV (1973), pp. 39–90
White, Leonard D., *The Jacksonians: A Study in Administrative History 1829–1861* (New York, Macmillan, 1956)
Wolff, Robert Paul, *The Poverty of Liberalism* (Boston, Mass., The Beacon Press, 1968)

Index

INDEX

For Product Safety Concerns and Information please contact our EU representative GPSR@taylorandfrancis.com
Taylor & Francis Verlag GmbH, Kaufingerstraße 24, 80331 München, Germany

www.ingramcontent.com/pod-product-compliance
Ingram Content Group UK Ltd.
Pitfield, Milton Keynes, MK11 3LW, UK
UKHW021956180926
475701UK00003B/60

* 9 7 8 0 4 1 5 6 1 1 5 1 0 *